Lecture Notes of the Institute for Computer Sciences, Social Informatics and Telecommunications Engineering   557

The LNICST series publishes ICST's conferences, symposia and workshops.

LNICST reports state-of-the-art results in areas related to the scope of the Institute. The type of material published includes

- Proceedings (published in time for the respective event)
- Other edited monographs (such as project reports or invited volumes)

LNICST topics span the following areas:

- General Computer Science
- E-Economy
- E-Medicine
- Knowledge Management
- Multimedia
- Operations, Management and Policy
- Social Informatics
- Systems

Der-Jiunn Deng · Jyh-Cheng Chen
Editors

Smart Grid and Internet of Things

7th EAI International Conference, SGIoT 2023
TaiChung, Taiwan, November 18–19, 2023
Proceedings

 Springer

Editors
Der-Jiunn Deng
National Changhua University of Education
Changhua, Taiwan

Jyh-Cheng Chen
National Yang Ming Chiao Tung University
Hsinchu, Taiwan

ISSN 1867-8211 ISSN 1867-822X (electronic)
Lecture Notes of the Institute for Computer Sciences, Social Informatics
and Telecommunications Engineering
ISBN 978-3-031-55975-4 ISBN 978-3-031-55976-1 (eBook)
https://doi.org/10.1007/978-3-031-55976-1

This Springer imprint is published by the registered company Springer Nature Switzerland AG
The registered company address is: Gewerbestrasse 11, 6330 Cham, Switzerland

Paper in this product is recyclable.

Preface

We are delighted to introduce the proceedings of the 7th edition of the European Alliance for Innovation (EAI) International Conference on Smart Grid and Internet of Things (SGIoT 2023). This year, it took place at the Windsor Hotel, TaiChung, Taiwan, during November 18–19, 2023. This conference provides an opportunity to connect with researchers, developers, and practitioners from around the world to discuss recent findings in the area of the emerging Smart Grid and Internet of Things. The technical program of SGIoT 2023 consisted of 15 full papers in oral presentation sessions at the main conference tracks.

These technical papers cover a broad range of topics in wireless sensors, vehicular ad hoc networks, security, deep learning and big data. Aside from the high-quality technical paper presentations, the technical program also featured two keynote speeches. The first keynote speech was entitled "Satellites as an Enabling Technology for Internet of Thing," by Mohammed Atiquzzaman, from University of Oklahoma, USA. The second keynote speech was entitled "Monitoring Internet of Things: challenges and optimizations," by Abderrahim Benslimane, from University of Avignon, France.

Coordination with the steering chair, Imrich Chlamtac, was essential for the success of the conference. We sincerely appreciate his constant support and guidance. It was also a great pleasure to work with such an excellent organizing committee team for their hard work in organizing and supporting the conference. In particular, the Technical Program Committee completed the peer-review process of technical papers and made a high-quality technical program. We are also grateful to the Conference Manager, Veronika Kissova, for her support and to all the authors who submitted their papers to the SGIoT 2023 conference.

We strongly believe that the SGIoT conference provides a good forum for all researchers, developers and practitioners to discuss all science and technology aspects that are relevant to smart grids and Internet of Things. We also expect that future SGIoT conferences will be as successful and stimulating, as indicated by the contributions presented in this volume.

November 2023

Der-Jiunn Deng
Jyh-Cheng Chen

Organization

Steering Committee

Al-Sakib Khan Pathan   United International University, Bangladesh
Der-Jiunn Deng   National Changhua University of Education, Taiwan

Organizing Committee

Honorary Chair

Pao-Tao Chen   Overseas Chinese University, Taiwan

General Chairs

Der-Jiunn Deng   National Changhua University of Education, Taiwan
Jyh-Cheng Chen   National Yang Ming Chiao Tung University, Taiwan

TPC Chairs and Co-chairs

Chun-Cheng Lin   National Yang Ming Chiao Tung University, Taiwan
Chien-Liang Chen   Overseas Chinese University, Taiwan

Sponsorship and Exhibit Chair

Hui Hsin Chin   Overseas Chinese University, Taiwan

Publicity and Social Media Chair

Hsiang-Yun Wu   TU Wien, Austria

Workshop Chair

Jun-Li Lu   University of Tsukuba, Japan

Local Chair

Rung-Shiang Cheng   Overseas Chinese University, Taiwan

Publications Chair

Yu-Liang Liu   Overseas Chinese University, Taiwan

Web Chair

Chien-Liang Chen   Overseas Chinese University, Taiwan

Award Committee/Student Travel Chair

Hai Dong   RMIT University, Australia

Technical Program Committee

Chun-Cheng Lin   National Yang Ming Chiao Tung University,
                                       Taiwan
Chien-Liang Chen   Overseas Chinese University, Taiwan
Chao-Yu Chen   National Cheng Kung University, Taiwan
Fan-Hsun Tseng   National Cheng Kung University, Taiwan
Sheng Tzong Cheng   National Cheng Kung University, Taiwan
Chin-Ya Huang   National Taiwan University of Science and
                                       Technology, Taiwan
Po-Hsuan Tseng   National Taipei University of Technology, Taiwan
Li Wang   Beijing University of Posts and
                                       Telecommunications, China
De-Nian Yang   Academia Sinica, Taiwan
Abderrahim Benslimane   University of Avignon, France
Kuan Zhang   University of Nebraska-Lincoln, USA
Jia-Chin Lin   National Central University, Taiwan
Alexey Vinel   Halmstad University, Sweden
Guangjie Han   Hohai University, China
Mohammed Atiquzzaman   University of Oklahoma, USA
Sherali Zeadally   University of Kentucky, USA

Naveen Chilamkurti   La Trobe University, Australia
Neeraj Kumar   Thapar University, India
Sergi Trilles Oliver   Institute of New Imaging Technologies, Spain

Contents

IoT, Communication Security, Data Mining and Big Data

Study on Anomaly Classifier with Domain Adaptation

Chien Hung Wu, Rung Shiang Cheng, and Chi Han Chen[✉]

Overseas Chinese University, Taichung City, Taiwan
{ludwig1017,rscheng}@ocu.edu.tw

Abstract. There are various characteristics of industrial defects, and there is no fixed pattern to search for. Typically, anomaly detection models are used to identify defects. However, after experiencing a domain gap, industrial defect images often lead to a decrease in the verification accuracy of the source model. We conducted experiments to validate this and employed a domain adaptation model. Using color transformation algorithms, we generated source images with domain gaps and introduced them to a pre-trained model. We trained the model to learn features from the source domain and utilized a domain discriminator to differentiate between features from the source and target domains, assuming that the mappings of the target and source domains come from the same distribution. Comparative experimental results demonstrate that the domain adaptation model has a significant impact on improving accuracy. Specifically, the accuracy of the original "flower" category increased from 43.98% to 89.23%, and the "cable" category improved from 75.33% to 85.66%.

Keywords: manufacturing defect · anomaly detection · domain shift · domain adaptation

1 Introduction

In the industrial sector, many production lines generate numerous defective products during the manufacturing process. Consequently, there are various models aimed at addressing this issue. These models fall into three primary directions: reconstruction-based methods [1, 2], synthesis-based methods [3, 4], and embedding-based methods [5, 6]. These trends have emerged to tackle the challenge of industrial defect detection. However, these three methods often place excessive emphasis on the authenticity of synthesis, which can lead to misjudgments due to model generalization after image reconstruction. The embedding approach, which involves substantial computation, frequently consumes excessive system resources, impeding the real-time applicability of models in industrial settings. In practical industrial environments, there are distinct production lines, yet products of the same category need to be distinguished as defective or not. Different machines introduce variations in lighting and color space transformations, making it necessary to identify corresponding defects in images of defective products.

D.-J. Deng and J.-C. Chen (Eds.): SGIoT 2023, LNICST 557, pp. 3–11, 2024.
https://doi.org/10.1007/978-3-031-55976-1_1

If the above-mentioned methods encounter domain shifts under various conditions in practical industrial settings [1–6], these three directions are prone to increasing the model's misjudgment rate [1–6]. Consequently, traditional defect detection methods are incapable of accurately identifying defective products.

Regarding the proposition made in [7], when dealing with differences in color spaces, the model exhibits a noticeable decrease in accuracy. This is an unreasonable outcome considering the expected results. Through data augmentation techniques like adjusting color and brightness, the overall performance of the model should not decline. During training, a model's capabilities are limited to what it has learned. Consequently, the model may lack the ability to clearly recognize features that it has not been trained on. Therefore, even when learning images within the same color space, merely adjusting brightness during validation can lead to a decrease in model accuracy [7]. In the industrial domain, domain shifts are quite common, especially when images are captured using different cameras and lighting sources. Images of defects from various machines within the same production line introduce a wide range of domain shifts. This severely restricts the model's ability to generalize and can even necessitate training a separate model for each source domain with different lighting conditions. When models need to adapt to different environments, it can result in misjudgments. Images transformed through changes in color space retain the original image's contour features. Thus, theoretically, this should not lead to a decrease in model accuracy. However, after training the model with source images and validating them with domain shift caused by changes in color features due to image algorithms, a noticeable decrease in accuracy is observed (Table 1).

In this work, we begin with the industrial defect dataset collected from MVTEC AD. Initially, we employ image color transformation algorithms to convert the original RGB target images into grayscale 1-channel source images. The transformed images introduce a domain gap in the source data, and the objective is to assess whether the accuracy of defect detection in the data remains intact after this domain gap is introduced. Following this assessment, in cases where a decrease in accuracy is observed, we explore methods to maintain the original level of accuracy. Leveraging existing open-source Domain Adaptation models, we design an approach that specifically addresses domain gaps related to color features in images. It's worth noting that our approach focuses solely on

Table 1. The verification accuracy of the domain gap images compared to the source image reveals a noticeable decrease in precision. The model, when validated with source data on domain gap images, experiences a significant drop in accuracy. The model is unable to use a single weight to distinguish between features from different domains.

Type	Source_data	Domain_gap_data
Model	Resnet-18	Resnet-18
Flower	70.83%	43.98%
Cable	93.24%	75.33%
Hazelnut	95.00%	86.04%
Pill	43.02%	67.53%

color space transformations and does not involve algorithms such as image binarization or image transparency. Through our methodology, models trained using this approach can be applied to a broader range of images that experience shifts in color space due to domain shifts.

2 Related Works

2.1 Anomaly Detection

[8] This paper introduces a memory-based segmentation network (MemSeg) for defect detection and localization on the surfaces of industrial products within a semi-supervised framework. MemSeg utilizes a U-Net as its foundational architecture and introduces artificially generated anomaly samples and memory samples from both distinct and common perspectives to assist the network's learning process. MemSeg also incorporates a multi-scale feature fusion module and a spatial attention module to more effectively coordinate memory information and high-level features from input images. MemSeg achieves state-of-the-art performance on the MVTec AD dataset, with image-level and pixel-level AUC scores of 99.56% and 98.84%, respectively. This paper addresses the issue of distribution mismatch between the source domain and target domain, which can arise when using a pre-trained model to extract image features. Therefore, this paper employs a custom anomaly simulation strategy to enhance the model's adaptability to anomaly detection tasks.

[9] Introduces a simple Convolutional Neural Network (CNN) architecture called SimpleNet for the detection and localization of abnormal regions in images in an unsupervised manner. SimpleNet comprises four components: (1) a pre-trained feature extractor responsible for generating local features, (2) a shallow feature adapter used to transform local features into the target domain, (3) a straightforward abnormal feature generator, employed to simulate abnormal features by adding Gaussian noise to normal features, and (4) a binary abnormality discriminator used to differentiate abnormal features from normal ones. During the inference phase, the abnormal feature generator is discarded. SimpleNet achieves state-of-the-art performance on the MVTec AD dataset, with image-level and pixel-level AUC scores of 99.6% and 98.1%, respectively. The paper mentions the issue of inconsistency between pre-trained features and the target domain, thus employing a feature adapter to reduce domain bias and enhance the model's adaptability to the target domain.

2.2 Domain Adaptation

[10] Used for unsupervised domain adaptation in deep neural networks. Domain adaptation refers to the process of training an effective classifier or predictor when the data distribution in the training and testing sets differs. The authors' approach involves adding a domain classifier to the standard forward network, which is responsible for distinguishing features from the source domain and the target domain. Then, through the backpropagation algorithm, they simultaneously minimize the label prediction error for the source domain and maximize the error of the domain classifier. This process makes

the features invariant to domain shifts. The authors also introduce a gradient reversal layer to facilitate this optimization. This method can be applied to any deep network trained using backpropagation and has demonstrated exceptional performance in various image classification experiments, surpassing previous unsupervised domain adaptation methods. However, this paper does not consider other types of domain shifts, such as variations in label distribution, task objectives, or data patterns.

[11] Introduces an unsupervised domain adaptation method based on adversarial learning called Adversarial Discriminative Domain Adaptation (ADDA). This approach allows for learning a feature representation of the target domain without requiring target domain labels, enabling effective classification of target domain data. Initially, a discriminative model is trained on the labeled source domain to learn a feature mapping and a classifier for the source domain. Subsequently, through adversarial learning, a feature mapping for the target domain is learned in such a way that it can deceive a domain discriminator, making it unable to distinguish between source and target domain features. Finally, during testing, target domain data is mapped to a shared feature space and classified using the source domain classifier. This method presents a unified framework that generalizes existing adversarial domain adaptation methods as different design choices and demonstrates its superiority through experiments. The approach outperforms existing methods in standard cross-domain digit classification tasks as well as a more challenging cross-modal object classification task.

3 Methods

(See Fig. 1).

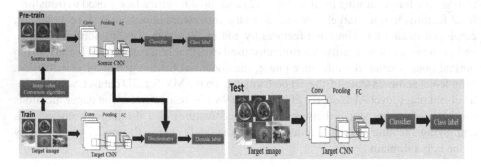

Fig. 1. Domain Adaptation model system architecture diagram

3.1 Generating Domain Gap Images

This paper focuses on the well-known MVTEC dataset in the field of anomaly detection and localization. An anomaly detection method is employed through a classification approach. Source images are generated using a color transformation algorithm applied to target images, which contain RGB color channels. No image binarization or transparency adjustment is conducted. The RGB chromaticity of the original images is transformed algorithmically to match the source images, which are then used to train a pre-trained model. Feature generation from both the source and target images can be referenced (Fig. 2), revealing a noticeable domain gap between the two, as illustrated in the figures.

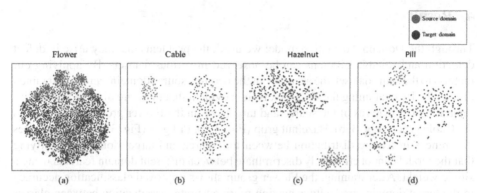

Fig. 2. The TSNE plot generated by the pre-trained model for (a) "Flower" (b) "Cable" (c) "Hazelnut" (d) "Pill" shows that the categories in the source and target do not overlap but gradually separate into distinct clusters. This plot serves as evidence that using a color transformation algorithm can indeed produce domain shifts.

3.2 Domain Adaptation Model

This paper verifies potential issues and a suitable solution for defect detection through a Domain Adaptation model. It begins by training a source model and processing target images through a color transformation algorithm to generate source images. The target images do not have labels. In the training phase, a pre-trained model is utilized to calculate classification losses, which are used to train the features and classifiers of the source domain. This ensures that they can correctly predict labels in the source domain. During training, two adversarial losses are employed. The first loss is computed by a discriminator to train a domain discriminator, enabling it to distinguish between feature mappings from the source and target domains. The second loss is used to train the target domain mapping, making it deceive the domain discriminator into thinking that mappings from the target domain and source domain originate from the same distribution. The objective is to align the feature spaces of the source and target domains. Once the feature spaces of the source and target domains are aligned, the model's recognition capabilities regarding images captured from different angles and color spaces are enhanced. This feature space alignment allows the model to adapt to various imaging scenarios.

3.3 Anomaly Detection with Classifier

Compared to performing segmentation for specific defects, using a classifier for defect detection offers greater versatility across various scenarios. Classifying the presence or absence of defects, as opposed to traditional anomaly detection, provides more flexibility in terms of applications. Through this experiment's design and verification, it is demonstrated that models trained on classifiers and through domain adaptation methods can enable the adaptation of the model to a wider range of scenarios and lighting conditions.

4   Result

Through the Domain Adaptation model we used, the problems that may arise in defect detection and suitable solutions can be observed in various datasets. By applying our method to the same dataset, the accuracy of the original source domain can be maintained (Table. 2). By examining the TSNE plots, it is evident that there are distinct boundaries separating the features of the source and target within the Flower group (Fig. 3. a) and the Cable group (Fig. 3. b), Hazelnut grop (Fig. 3. c), Pill grop(Fig. 3. d). This indicates differences in feature distribution between the source and target domains, signifying that the model cannot effectively discriminate between different domain features using a single weight. After training, the Flower group shows improved classification accuracy in the target domain, gradually achieving more accurate classification between classes (Fig. 4. a). Additionally, after training, the feature distributions become more similar, without a significant domain gap observed as in Fig. 2 and Fig. 4. However, in the case of cable, where color distinction is crucial for defect detection, the accuracy is maintained, but there is no clear classification in the TSNE plot (Fig. 4. b) (Fig. 4. c) (Fig. 4. d).

Table 2. Comparing domain-shifted images with source images to validate the accuracy in comparison to our method, using the same dataset. From the data that originally reduced accuracy by generating domain-shifted images, our method effectively maintains accuracy without decreasing it. Furthermore, after the domain shift, it can effectively enhance accuracy.

Type	Source_data	Domain_gap_data
Model	Resnet18	Resnet18
Flower	70.83%	43.98%
Cable	93.24%	75.33%
Hazelnut	95.00%	86.04%
Pill	43.02%	67.53%
Model	Ours	Ours
Flower	72.93%	89.23%
Cable	94.59%	85.66%
Hazelnut	90.00%	86.28%
Pill	63.95%	68.97%

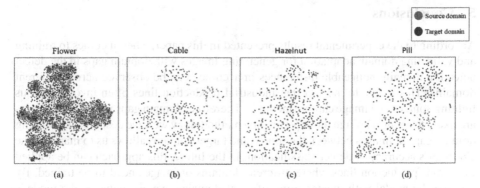

Fig. 3. Flower_Feature_TSNE(a) 、 Cable_Feature_TSNE(b) 、 Hazelnut_Feature_TSNE(c)
、 Pill_Feature_TSNE(d) (Red circles represent the source domain, and blue circles represent
the target domain). It can be observed through the red circles of the source domain and the blue
circles of the target domain that there is no clear boundary between the source and target. After
training, the features of the source and target gradually converge.

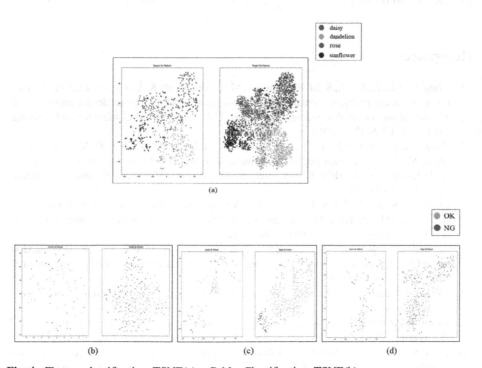

Fig. 4. Flower_classification_TSNE(a) 、 Cable_Classification_TSNE(b)
、 Hazelnut_Classification_TSNE(c) 、 Pill_Classification_TSNE(d) Through the TSNE plot
based on classification, it can be seen that the features between the source and target gradually
differentiate when compared for classification. Moreover, in terms of features (Fig. 2), they
gradually converge, indicating a reduction in the domain gap issue.

5   Conclusions

According to the experimental results presented in this paper, when it comes to training and validating domain adaptation for generating images with domain gaps in the defect detection domain, noticeable differences in accuracy can be observed across different domains. This is due to the fact that industrial production lines often involve various lighting sources and image capture methods. Therefore, domain gaps in captured images are likely to occur. Through the experimental methodology we have designed, simulating domain gaps in images between the source and target domains allows us to maintain the classifier's accuracy in defect classification. In the future, this approach can be applied to various production lines where different domains of images need to be trained. By training the model with images from different domains, we can enhance the model's ability to generalize across diverse scenarios.

Acknowledgment. The authors would like to thank the National Science and Technology Council, Taiwan, R. O. C. for financially supporting this research under Contract No. NSTC 112-2221-E-240-002-MY3.

References

1. Gong, D., Liu, L., Le, V., Saha, B., Mansour, M.R., Venkatesh, S., van den Hengel, A.: Memorizing normality to detect anomaly: Memory-augmented deep auto encoder for unsupervised anomaly detection. In Proceedings of the IEEE/CVF International Conference on Computer Vision, pp. 1705–1714 (2019)
2. Ristea, N.-C., Madan, N., Ionescu, R.T., Nasrollahi, K., Shahbaz Khan, F., Moeslund, T.B., Shah, M.: Self-supervised predictive convolutional attentive block for anomaly detection. In: Proceedings of the IEEE/CVF Conference on Computer Vision and Pattern Recognition, pp. 13576–13586 (2022)
3. Li, C.-L., Sohn, K., Yoon, J., Pfister, T.: Cutpaste: Self-supervised learning for anomaly detection and localization. In Proceedings of the IEEE/CVF Conference on Computer Vision and Pattern Recognition, pp. 9664–9674 (2021)
4. Zavrtanik, V., Kristan, M., Skocaj, D.: Draem-a discriminatively trained reconstruction embedding for surface anomaly detection. In: Proceedings of the IEEE/CVF International Conference on Computer Vision, pp. 8330–8339 (2021)
5. Defard, T., Setkov, A., Loesch, A., Audigier, R.: Padim: a patch distribution modeling framework for anomaly detection and localization. In: Del Bimbo, A., et al. (eds.) Pattern Recognition. ICPR International Workshops and Challenges: Virtual Event, January 10–15, 2021, Proceedings, Part IV, pp. 475–489. Springer International Publishing, Cham (2021)
6. Roth, K., Pemula, L., Zepeda, J., Scholkopf, B., Brox, T., Gehler, P.: Towards total recall in industrial anomaly detection. In: Proceedings of the IEEE/CVF Conference on Computer Vision and Pattern Recognition, pp. 14318–14328 (2022)
7. De, K., Pedersen, M.: Impact of colour on robustness of deep neural networks. In: 2021 IEEE/CVF International Conference on Computer Vision Workshops (ICCVW), Montreal, BC, Canada, 2021, pp. 21–30. https://doi.org/10.1109/ICCVW54120.2021.00009
8. Yang, M., Wu, P., Feng, H.: MemSeg: a semi-supervised method for image surface defect detection using differences and commonalities. Eng. Appl. Artif. Intell. **119**, 105835 (2023)

9. Liu, Z., Li, C.-L., Sohn, K., Yoon, J., Pfister, T.: SimpleNet: a simple network for image anomaly detection and localization. In: Proceedings of the IEEE/CVF Conference on Computer Vision and Pattern Recognition (CVPR) (2023)
10. Ganin, Y., Lempitsky, V.: Unsupervised Domain Adaptation by Backpropagation. In: International Conference on Machine Learning (ICML), pp. 1180–1189 (2015)
11. Tzeng, E., Hoffman, J., Saenko, K., Darrell, T.: Adversarial discriminative domain adaptation. In: Computer Vision and Pattern Recognition (CVPR) (2017)

Research on Federated Sharing Methods for Massive Data in Blockchain

Bing Wu and Haiyan Kang[✉]

School of Information Management, Beijing Information Science and Technology University,
Beijing 100192, China
kanghaiyan@126.com

Abstract. Data storage with the help of blockchain can ensure the transparency, non-tampering and autonomy of data information holders. However, the on-chain storage of massive data will seriously affect the performance of blockchain, and some private sensitive data and so on are not suitable for public storage in blockchain. To address the above problems, a trusted federated learning method based on local differential privacy mechanism, Loosely Coupled Local Differential Privacy Blockchain Federated Learning (LL-BCFL) is proposed for blockchain that realizes secure and efficient processing of massive user data. Firstly, a client selection mechanism is proposed and designed with the help of blockchain, which mainly includes two operations, namely, verification update and reputation calculation, to ensure the correctness and effectiveness of global model aggregation as well as the honesty and motivation of clients participating in training. Secondly, federated learning is used to realize the joint training of massive data distributed stored in each terminal device, so as to alleviate the phenomenon of "data silos" caused by privacy and security issues. In addition, a local differential privacy mechanism is designed in this method to solve the inference attack problem in the training process of federated learning. Finally, experiments are conducted on the MNIST dataset for both balanced and unbalanced datasets to verify the effectiveness of the proposed method LL-BCFL.

Keywords: Federated learning · Local differential privacy · Privacy protection · Blockchain storage · Massive data utilization

1 Introduction

In today's digital era, data is the core support and basic elements for the breakthrough development of emerging technologies and field industries such as artificial intelligence, cloud computing, mobile Internet and other big data industries. China has become the world's first data producer by virtue of the large amount of data generated from social networks, the Internet of Things, hospitals, banking systems, social networks, and other fields [1, 2], and the growth of data volume still shows explosive growth. The existence of massive data has provided fundamental guarantees for the development of various

D.-J. Deng and J.-C. Chen (Eds.): SGIoT 2023, LNICST 557, pp. 12–27, 2024.
https://doi.org/10.1007/978-3-031-55976-1_2

advanced technologies, but the increasing emphasis on data security and privacy protection by countries, enterprises, and individuals has led to the inability of massive data to be effectively shared and fully utilized [3, 4]. For example, data leakage, data theft and other data security issues caused by incidents such as the illegal and excessive collection and use of users' personal information by Didi Company, as well as the introduction of legal documents related to data privacy protection, such as the "Data Security Law of the People's Republic of China" and the "Personal Information Protection Law of the People's Republic of China", have all reflected the phenomenon of massive data being difficult to centrally process.

With the security attributes of blockchain such as traceability and tamperability, the secure storage of distributed data is effectively realized [5]. However, the on-chain storage of massive data will lead to a series of problems such as higher storage cost, slower transaction efficiency, and higher probability of node failure in blockchain. In view of the above blockchain massive data storage and the "data silos" problem caused by the distributed storage of massive data, it is proposed to adopt the idea of combining "on-chain and off-chain" to realize the efficient utilization and safe processing of massive data by combining with the federated learning technology [6]. In recent years, the model construction method combining blockchain technology and federated learning technology has been widely studied. For example, Qi et al. [7] proposed a federated learning framework based on federated blockchain to solve the security vulnerabilities and data privacy breaches caused by single point of failure, and ultimately realize the traffic flow prediction under privacy protection.

Federated learning is an effective solution to the privacy protection problem in machine learning, but there is still a risk of privacy leakage during its model training process [8–10]. With the help of federated learning technology to solve the "data silos" problem caused by industry competition, privacy security, and aggregation cost, while combining with the corresponding privacy protection methods to ensure the security in the model training process. In recent years, there are 2 main research directions on privacy protection techniques in federated learning, which are perturbation mechanism and encryption mechanism. The perturbation mechanism is mainly implemented by centralized differential privacy (CDP) and local differential privacy (LDP), which directly adds noise to the original data and perturbs sensitive information such as data features so that even if the data is leaked or stolen by a malicious attack, the valid information of the original data cannot be accurately inferred. Zhang et al. [11] applied the local differential privacy technique to the clustering problem and proposed AGCluster, a privacy-preserving grid clustering method based on LDP, to improve the quality of clustering under the premise of guaranteeing data privacy and security. Encryption mechanism is an indirect data privacy protection method acting in the process of data exchange, which is realized by combining security techniques such as cryptography tools, such as homomorphic encryption and secret sharing techniques. Yu et al. [12] proposed an efficient and secure federated aggregation scheme based on homomorphic encryption, which effectively solves the problems of federated learning data security as well as increased communication overhead after encryption.

The above related researches have made important breakthroughs in data processing and data privacy protection, but at the same time, there are still the following three urgent problems to be solved, which are (1) federated learning under massive data suffers from the problem of inefficient information retrieval from distributed data terminal and is not easy to be managed, (2) there may be dishonest and unresponsive malicious clients participating in the training of federated learning models, and (3) only the validity verification is considered on the balanced data sets, without considering the actual prevalence of unbalanced datasets, which lacks the universal validation of the proposed method. Through in-depth research on the above issues, the main contributions of this paper are as follows.

(1) Propose a trusted federated learning method based on local differential privacy mechanism for blockchain, i.e., Loosely Coupled Local Differential Privacy Blockchain Federated Learning (LL-BCFL), to achieve the effective utilization and efficient processing of distributed massive user data.
(2) Propose a client selection method for participating in model training to ensure the correctness and effectiveness of global model aggregation, as well as the honesty and enthusiasm of participating clients in training.
(3) Design a local differential privacy mechanism to act in the federated learning parameter passing process, and perturb the data by adding noise to solve the privacy leakage problem in federated learning model training.
(4) Considering both balanced and unbalanced datasets, a large number of experiments are performed on MNIST real datasets to evaluate the effectiveness of the proposed method.

2   Related Work

2.1   Blockchain

Blockchain, as a distributed ledger technology with security attributes such as transparency, non-tamperability, and non-repudiation [13], is widely used in various fields such as finance, healthcare, and public services [14, 15]. While blockchain technology shows great potential in various fields, it also faces the following 2 key issues [16], which are (1) security issue, and (2) scalability issue. The security of blockchain systems is ensured by cryptography and consensus algorithms, however, theoretical weaknesses in security mechanisms can lead to the possibility of malicious attacks on blockchain systems such as malware attacks, distributed denial of service attacks, and other malicious attacks. The three main reasons that contribute to the scalability issues [17] of blockchain systems include the following (1) low throughput, (2) excessive data load, and (3) inefficient query engines.

Massive data storage with the help of blockchain may cause problems such as transaction, query, and other functions become inefficient due to data overload. Therefore, it is considered to combine with federated learning to directly store massive data locally at each terminal, which solves the problem of data security and privacy protection while solving the problem of decentralized massive data usage.

2.2   Federated Learning

Federal learning (FL) [18] adheres to the core idea of "data does not move, the model moves, and the data is available but not visible", and trains machine learning models by combining data from multiple parties under the premise of not sharing local data. Combined with deep learning, privacy protection technology and other domain technologies, it solves the problem of maximizing the utilization of massive data under decentralized storage. The definition of federated learning is as follows.

Definition 1 Federated learning [19]. Define N participants $\{F_1, ..., F_N\}$ to hold their respective datasets $\{D_1, ..., D_N\}$ and collaborate to train a global model M_{FED}. Compared with the centralized traditional machine learning model M_{FED}, the federated learning model M_{FED} has a certain degree of accuracy loss. Let V_{FED} be the accuracy of the federated learning model and V_{SUM} be the accuracy of the traditional machine learning model, the loss of accuracy is

$$|V_{FED} - V_{SUM}| < \delta (\delta \text{ is a non } - \text{ negative real number}) \tag{1}$$

Ideally, the loss of accuracy of the federated learning model is small, i.e., the non-negative real number δ is small.

Federated learning better solves the problems of "data silos" and data privacy and security, but it still has the defects of reliability and security. Therefore, it is an important challenge for federated learning to solve the security problem of parameter transfer between the center server and the clients and the honest reliability problem of the clients participating in the model training by combining with relevant privacy protection techniques.

2.3 Local Differential Privacy Technique

In 2008, Dwork proposed the concept of differential privacy (DP), which mainly relies on a randomization algorithm. Differential privacy mechanism can be utilized to protect against differential attacks and inference attacks in order to prevent the attacker from successfully obtaining the specific information of a particular piece of data based on some small differences in information. In this paper, in order to ensure the availability of data, we utilize the relaxation differential privacy which is widely used in real world scenarios and is defined as follows.

Definition 2 (ε, δ)-Differential privacy [20].Given n users, for any randomized algorithm M, take as input any two neighboring datasets D and D' that differ by at most one record, such that any subset of the output of algorithm M be Y $(Y \in R)$ and satisfy.

$$Pr[M(D) = Y] \leq e^\varepsilon \times Pr[M(D') = Y] + \delta \tag{2}$$

Then the algorithm M is said to satisfy (ε, δ)-differential privacy. Where parameter ε denotes the magnitude of the degree of privacy protection, the smaller the value of ε the higher the degree of privacy protection. δ is a relaxation parameter to ensure the effectiveness of relaxed differential privacy, which is usually taken to be a small positive number, e.g., 0.1 or less.

Differential privacy is mainly realized by adding random noise to the input parameters or output results to perturb the data. Common data perturbation mechanisms [21] are Gaussian, Laplace and random response mechanisms. In particular, the Gaussian mechanism achieves (ε, δ)-differential privacy by adding normally distributed Gaussian noise with mean 0 and variance $\sigma^2 I$ to the output $f(t)$, i.e., $M(t) = f(t) + M(\sigma^2 I)$. The introduced Gaussian noise satisfies a Gaussian distribution and is a random number in the range between $(0, \sigma^2 I)$ and I for the unit matrix. The Laplace mechanism achieves (ε, δ)-differential privacy by adding to the output result $f(u)$ a Laplace noise generated according to the Laplace distribution of the probability density function $p(x|\lambda|) = \frac{1}{2\lambda} e^{-|x|/\lambda}$, i.e., $M(t) = f(u) + Laplace(\Delta f / \varepsilon)$, $Laplace(\bullet)$ is Laplace noise.

3 LL-BCFL Method Design

3.1 Description of the Problem

Storing massive data in the blockchain will exacerbate the problems of scalability, low throughput, and high latency efficiency of the blockchain itself, and distributed storage of large amounts of data across local users will exacerbate the phenomenon of "data silos", which leads to the inability to effectively utilize massive data. Federated learning technology is widely used to solve the centralized data collection and processing problems of traditional machine learning, but there are still privacy and security issues such as dishonest clients uploading false update parameters or intermediate parameter leakage in the model training process.

Therefore, in order to realize the effective utilization and efficient processing of massive data in distributed terminal devices while ensuring privacy and security, there is an urgent need to solve the above problems. The related symbols and parameters involved in this paper are shown in Table 1.

Table 1. Related symbols and parameters

Notation	Meaning
M	Number of clients
N	Number of federal learning participants
T	Total number of federated learning exchange rounds
ε	Privacy budget in local differential privacy definition
δ	Relevant parameters in local differential privacy definition
w_i	Model parameters relevant for client evaluation in federated learning
u_i	Client-trained local model

3.2 Local Data Query Privacy Protection Mechanism

To address the above problems, this paper combines blockchain technology to propose a trusted federated learning method based on local differential privacy mechanism, i.e.,

Loosely Coupled Local Differential Privacy Blockchain Federated Learning (LL-BCFL) to realize efficient processing of massive user data. The method adopts the core idea of combining "on-chain and off-chain", and is constructed by storing data summary information on the chain and storing and processing massive data off the chain, and its architecture is shown in Fig. 1, which mainly contains the following three methods, namely, (1) loosely coupled BCFL method, (2) federated learning method based on local differential privacy, and (3) massive data storage and processing method. The proposed method in this paper provides an effective solution to the problem of using massive data in industries such as healthcare, finance, and security, where data privacy requirements are extremely high.

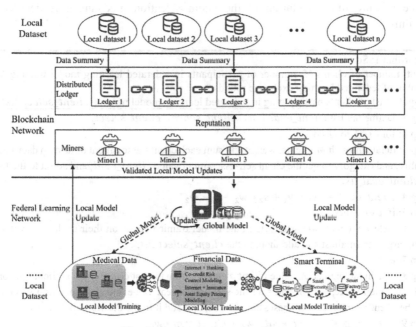

Fig. 1. System architecture diagram

3.2.1 Loosely Coupled BCFL Method

In this paper, the loosely coupled federated learning [22] approach is used to combine blockchain technology and federated learning mechanism, and its detailed coupling is reflected in Fig. 1. In particular, blockchain is used to validate model updates and manage the reputation of the client, which joins the federated learning network by sending down the reputation value. Federated learning based on server-client model is used for local model training and global model aggregation, joining the blockchain network by uploading local model parameter updates. In the loosely coupled BCFL, the distributed ledger is used to record information such as client data digests and reputation values, and the miners are used to provide a client selection mechanism for federated learning to select appropriate clients to participate in the model training process. The client selection process is described as follows.

(1) Client self-assessment: the client evaluates itself based on its data type, data size, and data type.
(2) Server evaluation: The server weights the client's self-assessment value and historical reputation value, and calculates the client's reputation index with the help of subjective logic model (SLM) method, and finally generates the client's comprehensive reputation value.
(3) Client selection: Select the clients as the participants of the federal learning model training according to the comprehensive reputation value in descending order.

The specific implementation of the client selection mechanism is detailed in algorithm 1.

Algorithm 1: Select_Client

Input: number of clients M, number of participants in federated learning model training N, number of federated learning exchange rounds T.

Output: List of clients participating in federated learning model training $client\_select\_list$.

Step 1: Define the list $client\_eval\_list$, $client\_score$, $client\_select$.

Step 2: for $i \leftarrow 1$ to M do

Step 3: Iterate through M clients, weight and sum each client's assessment of its own data size, quality, and category to get the client self-assessment value $client\_eval$, and add it to the list of $client\_eval\_list$.

Step 4: $client\_eval \leftarrow s_1 * w_1 + s_2 * w_2 + s_3 * w_2$

Step 5: if $t \leftarrow 1$ then

Step 6: Select N clients to participate in the model training based on their evaluation values from largest to smallest and add them to the $client\_select$ list.

Step 7: else

Step 8: Obtain the reputation value $client\_rep\_list$ from the list $client\_rep$ of client's historical reputation value, weight and sum the self-assessment value and the reputation value to get the client's comprehensive assessment value, and add it to the $client\_rep\_list$ list.

Step 9: $client\_rep \leftarrow client\_eval * w_4 + client\_rep * w_5$

Step 10: Select N clients to participate in the model training based on their comprehensive evaluation values and add them to the $client\_select\_list$ list.

Step 11: end for

Step 12: return $client\_rep\_list$

The client selection mechanism acts during each round of federated learning model training, iterating in a loop until the model converges. The server, with the help of the blockchain, selects reliable participants with high reputation for the federated learning task based on the client selection mechanism. The high-reputation participants bring with them high-quality data for modeling training, which can significantly improve the learning efficiency of federated learning. At the same time, the validation mechanism is provided for federated learning with the help of miners to verify the validity of local model updates. The validation update process is described as follows.

Obtain local model updates: the miner obtains the local model updates uploaded to the blockchain network by the client.

Validate model parameters: the miner validates the received local model updates according to predefined rules and constraints.

The implementation of the local model update validation mechanism is detailed in algorithm 2.

Algorithm 2: Valid_Model

Input: Updated client local model u_i, test dataset $valid\_data$, number of correctly predicted labels cor_num.

Output: Client local model accuracy acc.

Step 1: Prediction on updated local model u_i using validation dataset.

Step 2: $prediction \leftarrow u_i.\,predict(valid\_data)$

Step 3: Iterate through the prediction results and real labels, record the number of correctly predicted labels using accuracy as a performance metric, and thus judge the effectiveness of local model updates.

Step 4: $if\ prediction == valid\_data$:

Step 5: $cor\_num += 1$

Step 6: $acc = cor\_num\ /\ len(valid\_data)$

Step 7: return acc

After the miner completes the local model update validation mechanism, the validated model parameters are sent down to the server to ensure the validity and compliance of the local model update, to prevent malicious or invalid model parameters from entering the process of global aggregation, and to improve the reliability and overall performance of the models in the BCFL system.

3.2.2   A Federation Learning Method Based on Local Differential Privation

In this paper, we incorporate the local differential privacy mechanism into federated learning to solve the problem of possible inference attacks during intermediate parameter exchanges between server-side and client-side in federated learning. The method architecture is shown in Fig. 2, and its round of complete training process can be summarized as follows.

The central server is responsible for client selection and global parameter initialization, distribution, aggregation, and global model update. The selected clients get the global parameters and train the model locally by themselves. After that, the resultant parameters after adding noise perturbation are sent to the miners, who perform transaction validation to filter unqualified or even malicious local model updates [23], and calculate the reputation value to evaluate the reputation of the clients as the basis for the next round of client selection. The miner sends the verified local model updates and the reputation values of the clients to the server, which completes the final global model aggregation. This process iterates in a loop until the model converges.

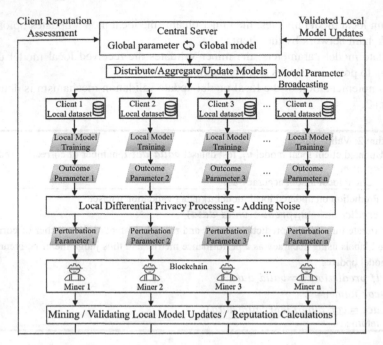

Fig. 2. A model structure for federated learning data sharing based on local differential privacy

3.2.3 Massive Data Storage and Processing Method

The storage of data in this system mainly includes the following two parts: (1) storage of simple data summary information on the blockchain, including local user informa-tion, dataset information, and client reputation value and other summary information, to ensure that the data stored on the chain is "visible and immutable", so as to facilitate the completion of the reputation calculation and client retrieval operations, and effectively improve data security and model training efficiency. (2) The storage of local datasets in the user terminal, which is directly managed by each data holder, provides a basic guarantee for data privacy and security. The processing of data in this system consists of the following three parts, namely, (1) the client uses the local data for model training and adds differential privacy noise to the process parameters, (2) uploads the trained local model updates to the miner for validation, and (3) sends the validated local model updates to the server for aggregation and sends the aggregated model parameters to the client.

3.3   Method Analysis

In the LL-BCFL method, the relevant data summary information is stored with the help of blockchain, and the unique properties of blockchain can ensure the security of the information. Secondly, the designed client selection mechanism can ensure the reliability and motivation of clients participating in model training. In addition, the introduction of local differential privacy mechanism can effectively avoid the problem of inference attacks that may be suffered during the training process of federated learning models. Therefore, the LL-BCFL method proposed in this paper has high security.

For the time complexity of the algorithm, the LL-BCFL method mainly consists of the aggregation algorithm of the server and the local model training algorithm of the client, and the local model training algorithm of the client as well as the Select_Client algorithm and the Valid_Model algorithm proposed in this paper are nested in the aggregation algorithm of the server. Denote the overall number of iterations of the LL-BCFL method is T., the number of participants is M, and the time complexity of the server's aggregation algorithm is $O(log(M))$ at each iteration, the time complexity of the LL-BCFL method is equal to that of the server's aggregation algorithm, which is $O(Tlog(M))$.

4 Experiment and Analysis

4.1 Experimental Environment and Dataset

Experimental Environment

This section evaluates the effectiveness of the modeling approach proposed in this paper and designs comparative experiments. The experiments are conducted under the operating system Windows 10 (64-bit), and the experimental code is implemented in the Pycharm development environment based on the programming language Python 3.8 for collaborative model training for federal learning. The hardware configuration is Intel(R) Core(TM) i5-8265U CPU @ 1.60GHz, NVIDIA GeForce MX150 GPU, 8 GB RAM. Deep learning models are trained using Pytorch 1.7.1 and differential privacy noise is added. The neural network model used for the network architecture of this experiment is conventional neural network (CNN) through which the global model is trained iteratively. The stochastic optimization algorithm used in this experiment is stochastic gradient descent (SGD) method, with which the model parameters are adjusted to iteratively optimize the local model.

Experimental Dataset

The MNIST dataset was chosen for training and testing in the experiment, which contains 10 grayscale images of handwritten digits 28×28 with 60,000 training samples and 10,000 test samples. The MNIST dataset is loaded automatically by code during the experiment to provide training data for the local model training of each participant as a way to simulate the horizontal federated learning process. The multi-party data used for federated learning suffers from variability issues due to factors such as domain-industry characteristics, which can have a direct impact on the accuracy and validity of the final model. Therefore, it is necessary to balance the data samples in the dataset before model training begins.

4.2 Model Effectiveness Evaluation Experiment

In this section, the effectiveness of the proposed method is evaluated by comprehensively considering both balanced and unbalanced datasets, using convolutional neural network (CNN) as the client's training model. Two parameter variables, namely the noise type and the number of training rounds, are mainly targeted to explore their effects on the global accuracy of the model, respectively. The two experiments are conducted on the MNIST dataset, and the main implementation methods are as follows.

(1) Explore the effect of noise type on the global accuracy of the model.

Under the differential privacy parameter C = 10% and participant N = 100, the added noise is set to be Laplace noise, Gaussian noise, respectively, and no differential privacy without adding any noise is used as a control to derive the impact on model accuracy produced by the addition of privacy noise.

1) Under the above conditions, the model is trained for 100 rounds using the balanced dataset and the results are shown in Fig. 3.

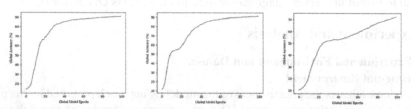

Fig. 3. Global accuracy with 100 rounds of IID distribution (left to right No-DP, Laplace-DP, Gaussian-DP)

2) Under the above conditions, the model is trained for 100 rounds using the unbalanced dataset and the results are shown in Fig. 4.

Fig. 4. Global accuracy with 100 rounds of Non-IID distribution (left to right No-DP, Laplace-DP, Gaussian-DP)

The following conclusions can be drawn from the curves obtained from the experiment, Figs. 3 and 4.

(1) Using a balanced dataset trained for 100 rounds with the same number of participants, adding noise affects the accuracy of model training. In particular, adding Laplace noise has little effect on the model accuracy and the final model accuracy reaches 90%. However, adding Gaussian noise has a greater effect on the model accuracy and the model accuracy reaches only 70% at the highest.

(2) Using the unbalanced dataset to train 100 rounds under the premise of the same number of participants, the curve fluctuates greatly compared to Fig. 3, and the final accuracy is reduced, and the addition of Laplace noise and Gaussian noise all appear

to be unable to converge. Therefore, under the condition of fewer training rounds using unbalanced dataset, adding noise can not complete the training of the model.
(3) Under the same training conditions, the model accuracy fluctuates greatly during model training using the unbalanced dataset, and its final accuracy decreases compared to model training using the balanced dataset. At the same time, the Gaussian mechanism differential privacy method for low latitude dataset under less rounds of learning has too much influence on the perturbation of the data, which seriously affects the model effectiveness and cannot be used.
(2) Explore the effect of the number of training rounds on the global accuracy of the model.

In the case of differential privacy parameter C = 10% and participant N = 100, the number of training rounds is set to 100, 200, and 500, respectively. Three cases of no differential privacy, Laplace mechanism differential privacy, and Gaussian mechanism differential privacy are considered to derive the impact of the number of training rounds on the accuracy of the model.

1) Under the above conditions, 100 rounds of training the model with balanced dataset and the results are shown in Fig. 3; 100 rounds of training the model with unbalanced dataset and the results are shown in Fig. 4.
2) Train the model for 200 rounds under the above conditions.

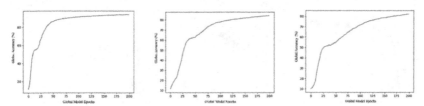

Fig. 5. Global accuracy with 200 rounds of IID distribution (left to right No-DP, Laplace-DP, Gaussian-DP)

Fig. 6. Global accuracy with 200 rounds of Non-IID distribution (left to right No-DP, Laplace-DP, Gaussian-DP)

Through the curves obtained from the experiment, Figs. 5 and 6, and combined with Figs. 3 and 4, the following conclusions can be obtained.

(1) Using a balanced dataset trained for 200 rounds with the same number of participants, the global model accuracy curves with the addition of two noises respectively have

roughly the same trend, and the final model accuracies are all between 80% and 90%.

(2) Using the unbalanced dataset with the same number of participants for 200 rounds of training, the final accuracies of the models are all reduced compared to Fig. 5. The federated learning curve graph with Laplace noise added in Fig. 6 has a 10% increase in final accuracy compared to the federated learning curve graph with Laplace noise added in Fig. 4. The federated learning plot with Gaussian noise added in Fig. 6 shows a significant improvement in training results compared to the federated learning plot with Gaussian noise added in Fig. 4.

3) Train the model for 500 rounds under the above conditions.

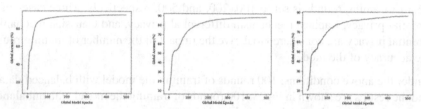

Fig. 7. Global accuracy with 500 rounds of IID distribution (left to right No-DP, Laplace-DP, Gaussian-DP)

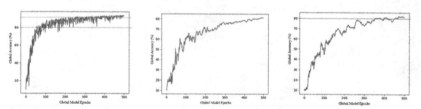

Fig. 8. Global accuracy with 500 rounds of Non-IID distribution (left to right No-DP, Laplace-DP, Gaussian-DP)

Through the curves obtained from the experiment, Figs. 7 and 8, and combined with Figs. 3, 4, 5 and 6, the following conclusions can be obtained.

(1) After 500 rounds of training with the same number of participants using the balanced dataset, the differences in the curves of the global model accuracy after adding the two noises separately become very small, and all of them have the characteristics of the curves obtained from the model training using the no-difference privacy technique at the early stage of training.

(2) Using the unbalanced dataset for 500 rounds of training with the same number of participants increases the final accuracies of the models compared to Fig. 6 for all of them, and the final model accuracies are almost the same compared to the results of Fig. 5 for 200 rounds of training using the balanced dataset.

(3) In the comparison of different number of training rounds using balanced dataset, the bounding curves of the federated learning accuracy under Laplace mechanism and

Gaussian mechanism both illustrate that increasing the number of training rounds of federated learning can improve the accuracy of the trained model. In the comparison of different numbers of training rounds using unbalanced datasets, unbalanced datasets that are prevalent in reality can be well aggregated into high-accuracy models as long as the number of rounds of training using federated learning is high enough.

5 Conclusions

In this paper, we combine blockchain technology and federated learning mechanism to propose and design a trusted federated learning method LL-BCFL based on local differential privacy mechanism to achieve secure and efficient processing of massive data. The blockchain is utilized to store simple summary information such as the personal information and reputation value of each local user, the type and number of entries of the data, to avoid storing too much data that affects the performance of the blockchain while improving the retrieval efficiency of user-related information. Design a selection mechanism for clients participating in model training, whereby clients are evaluated by miners in the blockchain through the verification of model update parameters and reputation calculation operations to ensure that honest and active clients are selected to participate in each round of model training, improving the efficiency and accuracy of model training. Federated learning is used to achieve centralized "sharing" of distributed massive data, and a local differential privacy mechanism is introduced to effectively ensure the security of parameter transmission during model training. Finally, the proposed LL-BCFL method is validated on the real dataset MNIST by conducting experiments on balanced and unbalanced datasets, and comparing with the original federated learning without differential privacy. Future work will focus on the integration of federated learning with advanced technological fields, as well as the study of privacy-preserving techniques in federated learning, in order to realize the improvement of the global accuracy of the resulting learning model while ensuring data privacy and security.

Acknowledgment. This work is partially supported by the National Social Science Foundation. China (No. 21BTQ079), the Humanities and Social Sciences Research Foundation of the Ministry of Education, China (No. 20YJAZH046), Beijing Advanced Innovation Center for Future Blockchain and Privacy Computing Fund, and Scientific Research Project of Beijing Educational Committee (KM202011232022).

References

1. Hu, J., Vasilakos, A.V.: Energy big data analytics and security: challenges and opportunities. IEEE Trans. Smart Grid **7**(5), 2423–2436 (2016)
2. Kang, H., Ji, Y., Zhang, S.: Enhanced privacy preserving for social networks relational data based on personalized differential privacy. Chin. J. Electron. **31**(4), 741–751 (2022)
3. Meng, X., Zhu, M., Liu, J.: Quantitative research on privacy risk of large-scale mobile users. J. Inform. Secur. Res. **5**(9), 778-788 (2019). (孟小峰,朱敏杰,刘俊旭.大规模用户隐私风险量化研究.信息安全研究, 2019, **5**(09): 778–788.)

4. Xiaofeng, M., Minjie, Z., Lixin, L., Junxu, L., et al.: Research on data monopoly and its governance modes. J. Inform. Secur. Res. **5**(9), 789–797 (2019). (孟小峰,朱敏杰,刘立新,刘俊旭.数据垄断与其治理模式研究.信息安全研究, 2019, **5**(09): 789-797.)

5. Wang, L.P., Guan, Z., Li, Q.S., et al.: Survey on blockchain-based security services. J. Softw. **34**(01), 1–32 (2023). (王利朋,关志,李青山等.区块链数据安全服务综述.软件学报, 2023, 34(01): 1–32.)

6. Yang, Q., Liu, Y., Chen, T., Tong, Y.: Federated machine learning: concept and applications. ACM Trans. Intell. Syst. Technol. **10**(2), 12 (2019)

7. Qi, Y., Shamim Hossain, M., Nie, J., Li, X.: Privacy-preserving blockchain-based federated learning for traffic flow prediction. Future Gener. Comput. Syst. **117**, 328–337 (2021)

8. Yin, X., Zhu, Y., Hu, J.: A comprehensive survey of privacy-preserving federated learning: a taxonomy, review, and future directions. ACM Comput. Surv. **54**(6), 1–36 (2021)

9. Yang, Q., Liu, Y., Chen, T., Tong, Y.: Federated machine learning: concept and applications. ACM Trans. Intell. Syst. Technol. **10**(2), 1–19 (2019)

10. Zhu, L., Han, S.: Deep leakage from gradients. In: Yang, Q., Fan, L., Yu, H. (eds.) Federated Learn. LNCS (LNAI), vol. 12500, pp. 17–31. Springer, Cham (2020). https://doi.org/10.1007/978-3-030-63076-8_2

11. Zhang, D.Y., Ni, W.W., Zhang, S., Fu, N., Hou, L.H.: A local differential privacy based privacy-preserving grid clustering method. Chinese J. Comput. **46**(02), 422-435 (2023). (张东月,倪巍伟,张森等.一种基于本地化差分隐私的网格聚类方法.计算机学报,2023,**46**(02): 422–435.)

12. Yu, S.X., Chen, Z.: Efficient secure federated learning aggregation framework based on homomorphic encryption. J. Commun. **44**(01), 14–28 (2023). (余晟兴,陈钟.基于同态加密的高效安全联邦学习聚合框架.通信学报, 2023, 44(01): 14–28.)

13. Zhou, Y., Wang, C., Xu, J., Hu, K., Wang, J.: Privacy-preserving and decentralized federated learning model based on the blockchain. J. Comput. Res. Dev. **59**(11), 2423–2436 (2022). (周炜,王超,徐剑,胡克勇,王金龙.基于区块链的隐私保护去中心化联邦学习模型.计算机研究与发展, 2022, 59(11): 2423-2436.)

14. Sergii, K., Silvio, R., Giada, S.: Blockchain Tree for eHealth. In: The Internet of Things, pp. 1–5 (2019)

15. Kushch, S., Castrillo, F.P.: Blockchain for dynamic nodes in a smart city. In: The Internet of Things, pp. 29–34 (2019)

16. Muhammad, N.M.B., et al.: A survey on blockchain technology: evolution. Architect. Secur. IEEE Access **9**, 61048–61073 (2021)

17. Wei, Q., Li, B., Chang, W., Jia, Z., Shen, Z., Shao, Z.: A survey of blockchain data management systems. ACM Trans. Embed. Comput. Syst. **21**(3), 1–28 (2022). https://doi.org/10.1145/3502741

18. Kairouz, P., McMahan, H.B., Avent, B., et al.: Advances and open problems in federated learning. Found. Trends Mach. Learn. **14**(1–2), 1–210 (2021)

19. Dwork, C., Lei, J.: Differential privacy and robust statistics. In: Proceedings of the 41st Annual ACM Symposium on Theory of Computing, pp. 371–380. Association for Computing Machinery, Bethesda (2009)

20. Wang, X.-S., Kang, H.-Y.: Research on noise addition and precision analysis in differential privacy. J. Lanzhou Univ. Technol. **49**(3), 94–103 (2023). (王骁识,康海燕.差分隐私中噪声添加与精度分析研究.兰州理工大学学报, 2023, **49**(03), 94–103.)

21. Tang, L.T., Chen, Z.N., Zhang, L.F., Wu, D.: Research progress of privacy issues in federated learning. Chinese J. Comput. **34**(01), 197–229. (汤凌韬,陈左宁,张鲁飞等.联邦学习中的隐私问题研究进展.软件学报,2023,34(01):197-229.)

22. Gu, T.L., Li, L., Chang, L., Li, J.J.: Fair federated machine learning and its design: a comprehensive survey. Chinese J. Comput. **46**(09), 1991–2024 (2023). (古天龙,李龙,常亮,李晶晶.公平联邦学习及其设计研究综述[J/OL].计算机学报, 2023, 46(09): 1991-2024.)
23. Kim, Y.J., Hong, C.S.: Blockchain-based node-aware dynamic weighting methods for improving federated learning performance. In: Asia-Pacific Network Operations and Management Symposium, pp. 1–4 (2019)

Utilizing Wearable Devices to Assess the Level of Fatigue System

Ding-Jung Chiang[1], Chia-Ling Ho[2], and Chien-Liang Chen[3]([✉])

[1] Department of Digital Multimedia Design, Taipei City University of Science and Technology, Taipei, Taiwan, Republic of China
djchiang@tpcu.edu.tw
[2] General Education Center, National Taipei University of Nursing and Health Sciences, Taipei, Taiwan, Republic of China
chialingho@ntunhs.edu.tw
[3] Department of Innovative Living Design, Overseas Chinese University, Taichung, Taiwan, Republic of China
clchen@ocu.edu.tw

Abstract. In recent years, with the rapid advancement of technology, smartwatches have emerged as an eye-catching accessory offering new and convenient features. In today's fast-paced world where individuals lead hectic lives and work under immense pressure, fatigue often takes its toll on their bodies. In this study, we have developed an APP software that integrates the built-in heart rate detection function of the watch with our proprietary heart rate variability analysis program. The aim is to determine whether the user is experiencing fatigue. Once the APP software detects a high fatigue state, it immediately alerts the user. This innovative solution is expected to enhance the quality of life for individuals who may be unaware of their fatigue levels while working.

Keywords: Wearable Device · Internet of Things · Heart Rate Variability

1 Introduction

Since 2011, smartwatches have been on the market and have made significant progress in terms of functions, especially in the field of smart sports watches. Currently, smartwatches primarily focus on collecting health information by tracking metrics such as calories burned, distance covered, and sleep monitoring. Many users rely on the data collected by their smartwatches to observe and manage their own health. With the inclusion of heart rate sensors, most smartwatches also offer real-time heart rate monitoring, allowing users to optimize their workouts and exercise routines. Moreover, this heart rate data can also be utilized for breathing exercises and relaxation techniques. Most of these features focus on fitness, but there is still room for improvement in detecting fatigue and addressing other health concerns.

© ICST Institute for Computer Sciences, Social Informatics and Telecommunications Engineering 2024
Published by Springer Nature Switzerland AG 2024. All Rights Reserved
D.-J. Deng and J.-C. Chen (Eds.): SGIoT 2023, LNICST 557, pp. 28–38, 2024.
https://doi.org/10.1007/978-3-031-55976-1_3

Newspapers and magazines have recently been drawing attention to the growing issue of overwork in the workplace. A recent research [1] report that working more than 49 h a week, experiencing a high psychological workload, and having young children or elderly people with disabilities at home are factors that increase the risk of fatigue. Over time, this can have a significant impact on work efficiency and overall health, potentially leading to chronic fatigue. Common symptoms of chronic fatigue include weakness, poor memory, and digestive problems such as peptic ulcers, stomach pain, and diarrhea. Fatigue slows down the brain's ability to respond to stimuli, reduces alertness, and manifests in other behavioral symptoms. Therefore, monitoring heart rate is crucial to assess fatigue levels, as several factors can significantly endanger the human body.

By combining the watch's built-in heart rate detection function with our innovative heart rate variability analysis program, this study determines the user's level of fatigue. It then issues a warning alert to the user through the developed APP software. This is expected to improve the quality of life of users who may be working without realizing that they are fatigued.

2   Related Work

Fatigue [2] is a normal physical and psychological phenomenon. Temporary fatigue is a common occurrence when individuals experience excessive workload, stressful environments, intense physical exertion, or even anxiety. However, with adequate rest, this fatigue typically dissipates within a short period of time. The most common causes of fatigue are irregular lifestyles or lack of sleep. Studying the issue of fatigue is crucial for several reasons. First, it significantly affects physical well-being. Prolonged periods of fatigue and stress can significantly increase the likelihood of developing heart disease and high blood pressure, since fatigue weakens the body's defenses and makes people more susceptible to disease. Second, it has profound effects on mental and emotional health. Fatigue can easily induce feelings of depression, anxiety, and irritability. Furthermore, it hampers concentration, memory, and decision-making abilities. When people are tired of doing important or dangerous tasks for a long time, it can affect their daily lives or lead to serious mistakes with potentially very bad results. When tired, people may experience symptoms such as depression, low self-confidence, anxiety, difficulty focusing, thoughts of suicide, restlessness, allergies, paranoia, fear, and difficulty sleeping. Numerous methods can be utilized to evaluate one's level of fatigue, with some being more subjective, such as the implementation of questionnaires.

There is also a physiological method to measure fatigue by analyzing data, particularly heart rate [3,4]. The heart rate serves as the primary measure of an individual's physical condition. As the term implies, it refers to the frequency of heartbeats. A typical resting heart rate for a healthy person ranges from 60 to 100 beats per minute, with an increase occurring during exercise. The heart rate is a physiological marker that fluctuates in response to bodily changes and varies based on one's physiological conditions. In the event of poor health, it is possible for the heart rate to rise.

Heart rate (HR) and heart rate variability (HRV) are important indicators of recovery and balance of the autonomic nervous system [5]. HR is an indication of the number of heartbeats per minute. HRV is the change in the time interval between successive heartbeats. HRV is a reflection of the activity of the autonomic nervous system and the balance between its sympathetic and parasympathetic divisions. A high HRV is considered a sign of good health, adaptability, and strength. On the other hand, a low HRV may be related to stress, illness, or overtraining. HRV is influenced by the activity of components of the autonomic nervous system that change during sleep or wakefulness. Technological advancements have revolutionized the creation of affordable wearable devices that can precisely measure and gather various biological data, such as HRV. These wearable devices include HR monitoring bands, smartwatches, and fitness trackers, specialized HRV monitoring devices, finger sensors, and optical HR monitoring technologies. We can use these wearable devices to collect HR data and analyze HR variability, allowing us to evaluate the user's autonomic nervous system activity at any time.

Smartwatches are increasing in popularity. However, HR monitoring bands and HRV monitoring devices can be influenced by exercise and surrounding noise. As a result, some researchers have begun exploring the use of smartwatches to track and analyze HRV. The research [6] examined the accuracy of PPG signals collected by Samsung Gear Sport smartwatches against medical grade chest ECG monitors. It focused on HRV parameters in the HR and time domains, as well as in the frequency domain. The study showed that satisfactory HR, time-domain HRV, low-frequency, and high-frequency parameters were obtained during participants' sleep, whereas being awake resulted in satisfactory AVNN and HR accuracy, with bigger errors in the remaining HRV parameters. The use of a smartwatch for measuring HRV was found to be a suitable alternative to ECG-based HRV, according to a study [7]. Smartwatches provide accurate measurements and allow the full range of HRV to be measured, including the low-frequency component. Although using HRV labeling that primarily evaluates short-term variability can be helpful, it is still necessary to exercise caution. Therefore, in the course of this study, we successfully determined the user's level of fatigue through a combination of the built-in HR detection function of the watch and our innovative HRV analysis program. The user is then alerted of a warning through the developed app software. The aim is to enhance the users' quality of life by assisting them in acknowledging and resolving fatigue, even if they are oblivious to it.

3   Methodology

A wearable smart watch is provided to the user for measurement in this study. The user can set the device up and start measuring HR to assess fatigue simply by connecting the watch to a mobile phone app. The user will then be able to be more aware of whether or not he or she is in a state of fatigue. The architecture of the system is shown in Fig. 1.

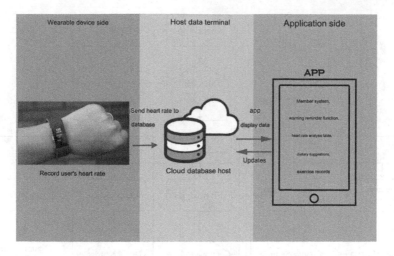

Fig. 1. The architecture of the system

The primary investigation of the study will be presented in three sections: first, developing the APP application program; second, creating a program to analyze HRV to assess fatigue status; and third, creating a program to offer nutritional guidance and record exercise.

3.1 APP Developing

To design the APP, this project is set to utilize the Java development environment of Android Studio. This includes the Java Development Kit (JDK) and the standalone Android Software Development Kit (SDK) tools. Additionally, MySQL will be employed to create a database for securely storing all relevant data. The system flow chart is shown in Fig. 2. The APP provides the following features.

A. **Member system**

To access the app page and its functions, registration as a member is necessary. Therefore, it is important to register as a member for the first time while using the app. This provides a reference for future comparisons when recording various heart rates and basic information. During registration, personal details such as name, age, height, weight, and other essential information should be entered for future reference in exercise and dietary calculations.

B. **Heart rate chart**

We have created a comprehensible chart for heart rate analysis, with monthly, weekly, and daily intervals for users to select from. Additionally,

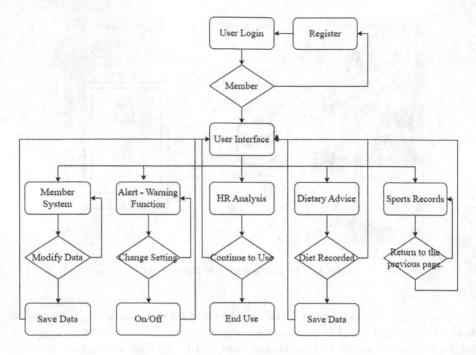

Fig. 2. System Flow Chart

users can choose a comfortable interface for analysis to conveniently check heart rate fluctuations.

C. **Warning alerts**

By analyzing the heart rate, it becomes evident whether the user is experiencing fatigue or not. Hence, this design sends vibration warnings to both the watch and the mobile phone when the user is fatigued, reminding them to take a break. The user can choose to enable or disable this function to prevent alert sounds from affecting his work during vital moments.

3.2   Developing a Program to Determine Fatigue

The study implemented a smartwatch to record the user's HR. After computing the RR interval, HRV analysis was performed utilizing the fast Fourier transformation technique to indicate the presence of fatigue in the user.

Table 1. Criteria for each band of heart rate variability

	Frequeny	Meaning
High Frequency (HF)	0.15 ~ 0.4 Hz	parasympathetic nervous activity
Low Frequency (LF)	0.04 ~ 0.15 Hz	sympathetic nervous activity
Very Low Frequency (VLF)	0.003 ~ 0.04 Hz	temperature homeostasis, partial parasympathetic control

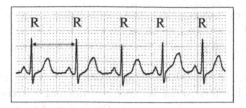

Fig. 3. The time between two neighboring R-waves

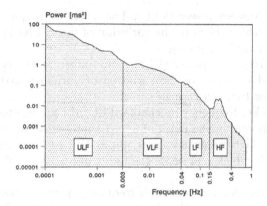

Fig. 4. Bandwidth of frequency domain analysis

A. Derive the RR interval

We use the HR tracking function of the smartwatch to automatically monitor HR. We then calculate the RR interval by using successive cycles of received heartbeats, subtracting the seconds corresponding to each R-value from the seconds of the previous point. The RR interval is shown in Fig. 3.

B. Heart Rate Variability Analysis

HRV analysis has two categories: time domain analysis and frequency domain analysis [5,8]. Time domain analysis is further divided into geometric and statistical methods. However, it is mainly used for long-term analyses. For immediate analysis, frequency domain analysis is preferred. The Fast Fourier Transformation (FFT) method is commonly used in frequency domain analysis. We utilized the Welch periodogram technique based on FFT [9] in this study to convert the time-series data into frequency data.

The continuous RR intervals are converted into the frequency domain using the Fast Fourier Transform during frequency-domain analysis, and the resulting spectral signals are carefully analyzed by the receiver. Based on Fig. 4 and table 1, we can deduce that frequency domain analysis encompasses the following metrics.

- Total power (TP): The intercepted frequency is less than 0.4 Hz, which refers to the variation of normal heartbeat intervals.

- High frequency power (HF): the intercepted frequency is from 0.15 to 0.4 Hz, which refers to the variation of normal heartbeat intervals in the high frequency range and represents the index of parasympathetic nerve activity.
- Low frequency power (LF): The intercepted frequency is from 0.04 to 0.15 Hz, which refers to the variation of normal heartbeat intervals in the low frequency range and represents the index of sympathetic nerve activity or the simultaneous regulation of sympathetic and parasympathetic nerves.
- Very low frequency power (VLF): The intercept frequency is from 0.003 to 0.04 Hz, which refers to the variation of normal heartbeat intervals in the very low frequency range.
- Ultra low frequency power (ULF): The intercept frequency is less than 0.003 Hz, which refers to the variation of normal heartbeat intervals in the ultra low frequency range.
- Normalized low frequency (normalized LF, nLF): refers to LF/(TP - VLF) × 100, representing the index of sympathetic nerve activity.
- Normalized high frequency (normalized HF, nHF): refers to HF/(TP - VLF) × 100, which represents the index of parasympathetic nerve activity.
- LF/HF stands for low and high frequency power ratio: an indicator of sympathetic/parasympathetic balance or an indicator of sympathetic regulation.

The standard established by the aforementioned method is utilized as a fatigue index, based on the balance between sympathetic and parasympathetic indexes.

3.3 Developing Dietary Advice and Exercise Logging Programs

A. Dietary Advice

A study [10] showed that a moderate amount of vitamin C supplementation can stabilize emotions, including fatigue, depression, insomnia, stress, overeating, anger, and other negative emotions were reduced by 35%. The nutritionist at the medical center has also provided a diet to help alleviate fatigue. They suggested specific foods from the following food categories, which are listed in the Table 2 below.

Table 2. Dietary Tips for Combating Fatigue

Category	Category Description
Complex Carbohydrates	Brown Rice, Whole Grain Bread, Mixed Grain Bread
Vitamin B12	Clams, Dried Small Fish, Oysters, Pork Liver, Salmon, Snapper, Swordfish
Folate	Wheat germ, Dark green vegetables (e.g. spinach, asparagus, cauliflower, mustard greens), Soybeans, Chicken liver
Iron	Brown sugar, Black sesame, Dried oysters, Wolfberries, Red cabbage, Red beans, Black beans
Vitamin C	Bell Pepper, Mung Bean Sprouts, Kiwi Fruit, Pomegranate, Papaya, Cauliflower, Tomato
Zinc	Oysters, Pumpkin seeds, Sunflower seeds, Pine nuts, Cashews
Magnesium	Pumpkin seeds, Sunflower seeds, Dark green vegetables

Rather than relying on coffee and soft drinks to support a tired body, we will provide advice on how to improve the diet by matching it with the appropriate dietary menu. Users can also upload their dietary records to calculate their daily calorie intake, so they can see which part of their intake is too much or too little and alert themselves.

B. **Sports Records**

According to research conducted by [11], it has been demonstrated that exercise may be an effective solution for improving chronic fatigue syndrome. Therefore, an interface will be set up to allow users to use the exercise animation provided by the app directly in the system to briefly stretch their muscles and bones, achieve the effect of exercise and record it in the app. In addition, this interface will provide feedback activities to allow users to complete tasks and provide rewards for success to motivate users to exercise. This project is expected to provide several exercise instructions, such as: stress relief yoga, walking, eye care exercise, etc., without having to go to the sports centre can also be implemented.

4   Results

We use the smartwatch to monitor HR and transmit data to a remote database. Subsequently, we employed a developed app to retrieve the HR data from the database and provide real-time analysis of the user's fatigue level. The app features a user-friendly interface and intuitive operation, allowing users to accurately determine their fatigue state.

The HR data, which are obtained from a smartwatch, represents the number of heartbeats per minute. This particular parameter plays a crucial role in assisting medical professionals in evaluating an individual's overall cardiovascular health. Using these HR data, we employ Eq. 1 to calculate the time elapsed between consecutive R peaks, which serves as a significant measure of HR variability. The RR period signifies the time interval between two consecutive heartbeats and is closely correlated with HRV. HRV, in turn, refers to the temporal

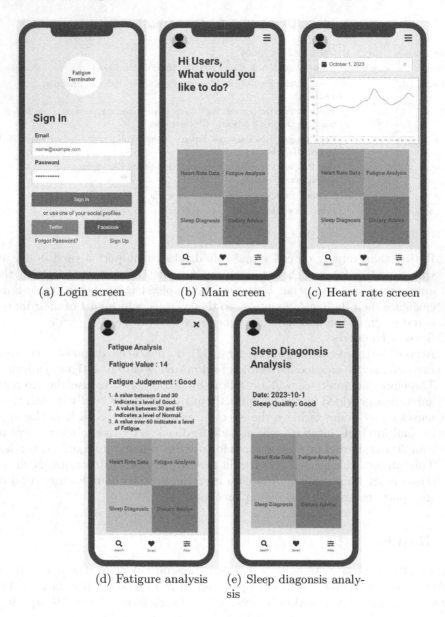

(a) Login screen   (b) Main screen   (c) Heart rate screen

(d) Fatigure analysis   (e) Sleep diagonsis analysis

Fig. 5. The screen of APP

fluctuation that occurs between successive heartbeats and provides insight into the adaptability and responsiveness of the cardiovascular system. It is a widely-used method for assessing the health and functionality of the cardiovascular system.

$$RR \text{ interval (ms)} = 60000/HR \tag{1}$$

If the heart rate is 60 beats per minute (BPM), then the RR interval would be 1000 milliseconds (ms). This indicates that there is a 1,000-ms (or 1 s) gap between consecutive heartbeats when the heart rate is 60 BPM.

We utilized the Welch periodogram technique, which is based on the Fast Fourier Transform (FFT), to convert the time series data into frequency data. The continuous RR intervals were transformed into the frequency domain using the FFT method during the frequency domain analysis, and the resulting spectral signals were analyzed meticulously. Welch's method is a valuable approach for estimating spectral density. It entails segmenting the data, applying a windowing technique, performing FFT computations, calculating the power, and then averaging the results. Next, we calculate the spectral parameters. These parameters often consist of the low-frequency and high-frequency components, which are associated with sympathetic and parasympathetic nervous system activity, respectively. Once we have the spectral parameters, we analyze the HRV results. We compare the LF, HF, and LF/HF values with established reference ranges to assess the individual's autonomic balance and overall HRV status.

The login screen for the APP program is displayed in Fig. 5(a). The main screen of the APP program can be seen in Fig. 5(b). In Fig. 5(c), we have the Heart Rate screen. The fatiguing analysis screen is shown in Fig. 5(d). Lastly, the sleep diagnosis analysis is presented in Fig. 5(e).

5 Conclusion

We are exploring the revolutionary use of wearable smartwatches to detect and notify users of their fatigue levels. Our research focuses on developing an app software that seamlessly integrates with the heart rate detection feature of smartwatches. By analyzing heart rate variability, we can identify signs of fatigue. Smartwatches have been monitoring health metrics since 2011. We can use them to address the problem of fatigue. Our aim is to improve people's well-being by warning them in advance about possible fatigue, particularly when they may not realize that their energy is decreasing while they are working or going about their daily activities.

Acknowledgments. This research is supported by National Science and Technology Council of Taiwan, under research Project NSTC 112-2221-E-240-003.

References

1. Chang, Y.: Distribution and correlates of burnout among paid employees in Taiwan. Taiwan J. Public Health **26**(1), 75 (2007)
2. Aaronson, L.S., et al.: Defining and measuring fatigue. Image J. Nurs. Scholarsh. 31(1), 45–50 (1999)
3. Al-Libawy, H., Al-Ataby, A., Al-Nuaimy, W., Al-Taee, M.A.: HRV-based operator fatigue analysis and classification using wearable sensors. In: 2016 13th International Multi-Conference on Systems, Signals & Devices (SSD), pp. 268–273. IEEE (2016)

4. Lu, K., Dahlman, A.S., Karlsson, J., Candefjord, S.: Detecting driver fatigue using heart rate variability: a systematic review. Accid. Anal. Prev. **178**, 106830 (2022)
5. Shaffer, F., Ginsberg, J.P.: An overview of heart rate variability metrics and norms. Front. Public Health 258 (2017)
6. Sarhaddi, F., et al.: A comprehensive accuracy assessment of Samsung smartwatch heart rate and heart rate variability. PLoS ONE **17**(12), e0268361 (2022)
7. Theurl, F., et al.: Smartwatch-derived heart rate variability: a head-to-head comparison with the gold standard in cardiovascular disease. Eur. Heart J.-Digit. Health **4**(3), 155–164 (2023)
8. Malik, M., et al.: Heart rate variability: standards of measurement, physiological interpretation, and clinical use. Eur. Heart J. **17**(3), 354–381 (1996)
9. Kamath, M.V., Watanabe, M., Upton, A.: Heart rate variability (HRV) signal analysis: clinical applications (2012)
10. Carr, A.C., Bozonet, S.M., Pullar, J.M., Vissers, M.C.: Mood improvement in young adult males following supplementation with gold kiwifruit, a high-vitamin C food. J. Nutr. Sci. **2**, e24 (2013)
11. Clauw, D.J.: Guided graded exercise self-help as a treatment of fatigue in chronic fatigue syndrome. Lancet **390**(10092), 335–336 (2017)

Task Offloading Method for Industrial Internet of Things (IIoT) Targeting Computational Resource Management

Wenhui Wang[1]([✉]), Xuanzhe Wang[1], Zhenjiang Zhang[1], and Zeng Jianjun[2]

[1] Beijing Jiaotong University, Shangyuan Village, Haidian District, No.3, Beijing, China
23111039@bjtu.edu.cn
[2] Beijing InchTek Technology, 1 Baiziwan South Road, Beijing, China

Abstract. In the context of industrial scenarios, devices exhibit specificity and task arrival rates vary over time. Considering real-world task queuing issues and incorporating edge computing offloading and D2D offloading techniques, this paper proposes TVTAO for computational resource management to meet latency requirements. First, three offloading decisions are introduced, then offloading policy constraints are proposed to restrict devices from selecting the same task for execution during task offloading. Simulation results demonstrate that the TVTAO algorithm can reasonably make task offloading decisions and allocate computational resources, effectively reducing the average processing latency of the overall system.

Keywords: edge computing offloading · D2D offloading · time-varying task offloading · deep reinforcement learning

1 Introduction

In an Industrial Internet of Things (IIoT) setting, intelligent devices often need to handle latency-sensitive and computationally intensive tasks, yet they have limited computational resources [1]. Task offloading strategies can be employed to transfer tasks to nearby edge computing servers or other intelligent devices for processing, thereby reducing the system's task latency [2]. However, real-world scenarios present challenges such as limited computational resources, varying task arrival rates [3], and device heterogeneity in the design of system policies. To address these issues, the paper proposes an offloading algorithm called TVTAO, utilizing deep reinforcement learning in conjunction with DDPG to find near-optimal solutions [4].

Given the challenges of dealing with numerous intelligent devices and various offloading constraints, this paper introduces the TVTAO offloading algorithm. It employs deep reinforcement learning to model the overall offloading strategy, aiming to find near-optimal solutions [5]. This algorithm effectively addresses the constraints posed by limited computational resources, fluctuating task arrival rates, and device heterogeneity in the context of the Industrial Internet of Things [6], resulting in a significant improvement in the overall service quality and reduction of task latency within the system [7].

D.-J. Deng and J.-C. Chen (Eds.): SGIoT 2023, LNICST 557, pp. 39–44, 2024.
https://doi.org/10.1007/978-3-031-55976-1_4

2 System Model

This paper considers an industrial Internet of Things (IIoT) scenario involving an Edge Computing Server (ESC) and multiple intelligent devices [8]. Within this scenario, intelligent devices can take on two roles: Computing Resource Consumer (CRC) and Computing Resource Provider (CRP) [9], as is shown in Fig. 1. CRC refers to an intelligent device that offloads some or all of its local tasks to other devices [10], requiring additional computing resources from these devices to complete its tasks efficiently, while Computing Resource Provider (CRP) is an intelligent device that executes its local tasks entirely within its own computing resources and may potentially offer computing resources to other devices [11].

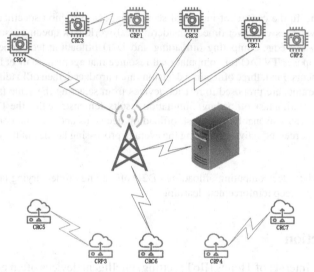

Fig. 1. Industrial Internet edge computing and D2D task offloading scenario

Assuming there are M intelligent devices in the scenario, a Base Station(BS) and an Edge Computing Server (ESC) [12]. The system proceeds through several time slots, with the intelligent devices making their offloading decisions within a single time slot. These offloading decisions primarily consist of three options: local computation, D2D offloading and edge computing offloading [13].

The status of whether device m offloads a task to the ESC in time slot t is represented by $\beta_t^{m,n} \in \{0, 1\}$, $\beta_t^{m,n} = 1$ represents that device m offloads tasks to device n, $\beta_t^{m,m} = 1$ represents that device m is CRP [14]. The offloading decision of device m with respect to D2D can be represented as formula 1:

$$\beta_t^m = \{\beta_t^{m,1}, \beta_t^{m,2}, \ldots, \beta_t^{m,M}\}^T, m \in \mathcal{M} \tag{1}$$

3   Methods

To address the optimization problem in the context of task offloading for IIoT devices, it is essential to consider mathematical model information such as the system's channel conditions and statistical distributions. However, in practice, obtaining this information is often unfeasible. Therefore, we have adopted an online solution based on deep reinforcement learning. This approach enables real-time resource allocation through interaction with the system, effectively making decisions regarding task offloading [15]. We have designed state spaces, action spaces, and reward functions, and proposed a time-varying task offloading algorithm based on edge computing and D2D, allowing the system to reduce overall system latency.

3.1   Notation

The system state is regarded as a set of parameters that can be used to describe the system. Based on the system model proposed in this paper, the system state at any time slot t is defined as formula 2:

$$s_t = \{A_t, T^r_{SD,t}, T^r_{ESC,t}\} \tag{2}$$

while A_t represents the number of tasks, $T^r_{SD,t}$ represents the remaining task execution latency of intelligent devices, $T^r_{ESC,t}$ represents that of edge server.

Based on the observed system state s_t, deep reinforcement learning will select an action based on decision variables, which can be represented as formula 3:

$$act_t = \{\alpha_t, \beta_t, o_t, f_{ESC,t}\} \tag{3}$$

while α_t represents the device makes offload decision or not, β_t represents the device performs full local computation or not, o_t represents the number of tasks.

The reward function is designed as the negative of the system latency, as is shown in formula 4:

$$r_t = \mathcal{R}(s_t, a_t) = -T_t \tag{4}$$

3.2   Task Offload Algorithm

This article combines the DDPG algorithm with real-world Industrial Internet of Things scenarios and proposes the TVTAO algorithm, as illustrated in the algorithm process shown in Table 1.

Table 1. The description of TVTAO training algorithm

Input: $K_{max}, T_{max}, |\mathcal{R}_B|, B, \lambda^Q, \lambda^\mu, C^Q, C^\mu$

1   Randomly initialize $Q(s,a|\theta^Q)$, $\mu(s|\theta^\mu)$, $Q'(s,a|\theta^{Q'})$ and $\mu'(s|\theta^{\mu'})$, $\theta^{Q'} \leftarrow \theta^Q$, $\theta^{\mu'} \leftarrow \theta^\mu$。

2   Reset $\mathcal{R}_B$.

3   **For** each eposide $k = 1,2,\dots,K_{max}$:

4   Randomly set an initial state s_1。

5   **For** each step $t = 1,2,\dots,T_{max}$:

6            $a_t = \mu(s|\theta^\mu) + \Delta\mu$。

7   Do action a_t and observe reward $r_t = \mathcal{R}(s_t, a_t) = -T_t$ and new state s_{t+1}.

8   Put transition(s_t, a_t, r_t, s_{t+1}) in $\mathcal{R}_B$. Drop the oldest sample if $\mathcal{R}_B$ is full.

9   Randomly select B transitions(s_t, a_t, r_t, s_{t+1}) as mini-batch。

10   **For** each transition $b = 1,2,\dots,B$:

11   Calculate $y^{(b)} = r_i^{(b)} + \gamma Q'(s_{i+1}^{(b)}, \mu'(s_{i+1}^{(b)}|\theta^{\mu'})|\theta^{Q'})$。

12   **End For**

13   Update $Q(s,a|\theta^Q)$ by $\theta^Q \leftarrow \theta^Q - \lambda^Q \nabla_{\theta^Q} L^Q$, while loss function is defined as $L^Q = \frac{1}{B}\sum_{b=1}^{B}[y^{(b)} - Q(s_i^{(b)}, a_i^{(b)}|\theta^Q)]^2$。

14   Update $\mu(s|\theta^\mu)$ by $\theta^\mu \leftarrow \theta^\mu - \lambda^\mu \nabla_{\theta^\mu} J^\mu$, while loss function is defined as $J^\mu = E_{s,a}[Q^\mu(s,a)]$, and:

$$\nabla_{\theta^\mu} J^\mu \approx \frac{1}{B}\sum_{b=1}^{B} \nabla_a Q\left(s_i^{(b)}, a\big|\theta^Q\right)\big|_{a=a_i^{(b)}} \times \nabla_{\theta^\mu}\mu\left(s_i^{(b)}\big|\theta^\mu\right)$$

15   Update parameters $\theta^{Q'} = \theta^Q$, $\theta^{\mu'} = \theta^\mu$ every C^Q and C^μ steps, respectively.

16   **End For**

17   **End For**

Output: approximate optimal policy μ^*

---

4   Simulation Results

Due to the inclusion of two types of intelligent tasks with different CPU cycles, the setting of CPU cycles is based on the original task CPU cycle setting, with a relative increase or decrease. The specific relationship is shown in Fig. 2.

Due to the inclusion of two types of intelligent tasks with different CPU cycles, the setting of CPU cycles is based on the original task CPU cycle setting, with a relative increase or decrease. The specific relationship is shown in Fig. 2.

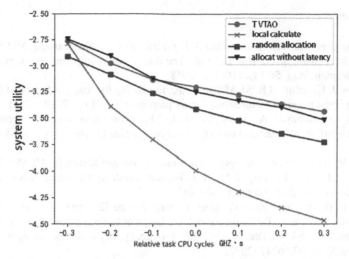

Fig. 2. The relationship between system utility and the number of CPU cycles

It can be seen that as the number of CPU cycles in a task increases, the system utility decreases. This is because as the number of CPU cycles increases, the task execution time becomes longer and the queuing delay also increases. Local computing significantly reduces system utility due to task accumulation on local devices; Random allocation can randomly use edge computing server and other device resources, so the system utility decline is less than that of local computing. The TVTAO algorithm can analyze the queuing delay and computing resource status of the current system environment. Compared to other strategies, it can choose the optimal offloading strategy to achieve higher system utility when the number of CPU cycles in the task changes.

5 Conclusion

This paper investigates the problem of managing computational resources for multiple tasks in the context of resource-constrained intelligent devices within an Industrial Internet of Things (IIoT) scenario. Firstly, considering the entire IIoT scenario, three offloading decisions are proposed: local computation, D2D offloading, and edge offloading. Secondly, to simulate the varying number of tasks due to factors like geographic location in industrial scenarios, a task offloading algorithm named TVTAO, based on deep deterministic policy gradients, is proposed to handle time-varying task arrivals. Finally, experiments and simulations are conducted using the PyTorch framework. The simulation results demonstrate that the algorithm performs exceptionally well in complex industrial scenarios.

References

1. Mohri, M, Rostamizadeh A, Talwalkar A. Foundations of machine learning. MIT press, 2018
2. Hassan, N., Gillani, S., Ahmed, E., et al.: The role of edge computing in internet of things. IEEE Commun. Mag. **56**(11), 110–115 (2018)
3. S. Caldas, J. Konečny, H.B. McMahan, et al.: Expanding the reach of federated learning by reducing client resource requirements. arXiv preprint arXiv:1812.07210 (2018)
4. Hsieh, K., Phanishayee, A., Mutlu, O., et al.: The non-iid data quagmire of decentralized machine learning. In: International Conference on Machine Learning, pp. 4387–4398. PMLR (2020)
5. Mining, W.: Data mining: concepts and techniques. Morgan Kaufinann **10**, 559–569 (2006)
6. Smith, V., Chiang, C.K., Sanjabi, M., et al.: Federated multi-task learning. Advances in neural information processing systems, p. 30 (2017)
7. LeCun, Y., Bengio, Y., Hinton, G.: Deep learning. Nature **521**(7553), 436–444 (2015)
8. Krizhevsky, A., Hinton, G.: Learning multiple layers of features from tiny images (2009)
9. Schulman, J., Wolski, F., Dhariwal, P., et al. Proximal policy optimization algorithms. arXiv preprint arXiv:1707.06347 (2017)
10. Caruana, R.: Multitask learning. Mach. Learn. **28**, 41–75 (1997)
11. Hanzely, F., Richtárik, P.: Federated learning of a mixture of global and local models. arXiv preprint arXiv:2002.05516 (2020)
12. Ruder, S.: An overview of multi-task learning in deep neural networks. arXiv preprint arXiv: 1706.05098 (2017)
13. Watkins, C.J.C.H., Dayan, P.: Q-learning. Mach. Learn. **8**, 279–292 (1992)
14. Ghosh, A., Hong, J., Yin, D., et al.: Robust federated learning in a heterogeneous environment. arXiv preprint arXiv:1906.06629 (2019)
15. Jie, Y., Guo, C., Choo, K.K.R., et al.: Game-theoretic resource allocation for fog-based industrial internet of things environment. IEEE Internet of Things J. **7**(4), 3041–3052 (2020)

Research on Vehicle Networking Resource Management Based on Trust Model in Intersection Scene

Yanyi Li, Zhaonian Li, Wenhui Wang, and Zhenjiang Zhang(✉)

Beijing Jiaotong University, No. 3, Shangyuan Village, Haidian District, Beijing, China
zhangzhenjiang@bjtu.edu.cn

Abstract. Recently, the traditional cloud computing network of vehicle networking has some problems to be solved: 1) the security trust between the vehicle and the subgrade unit; 2) The vehicle may be attacked by potentially malicious edge servers during task unloading. In this paper, in order to solve the above problems, aiming at the security problem of the edge computing network in the vehicle task unloading and resource allocation problems of multi-vehicle and multi-subgrade units in the urban intersection scene, the vehicle task unloading and resource management optimization algorithm and trust model based on the vehicle edge computing network are constructed, and the approximate optimal simulation is carried out for the urban intersection scene. Simulation results show that the proposed algorithm can effectively improve the overall efficiency of the system.

Keywords: Internet of Vehicles · Edge Computing · Resource Allocation · Trust Model · Reinforcement Learning

1 Introduction

Nowadays, the introduction of edge computing unit in vehicle networking has some problems to be solved in practical application scene [1]. The first is the security and trust issues between the vehicle and the subgrade unit. When the malicious subgrade unit maliciously interferes with the vehicle, it will greatly affect the service quality of the vehicle edge computing network. On the other hand, the computing resources and energy resources in the subgrade processing unit are relatively limited and dynamic, so when the vehicle is attacked by malicious edge servers during the unloading process, the resource competition between vehicles will be more intense and unstable.

Based on the analysis of the trust problem and resource allocation problem between vehicles and subgrade units in road intersection scene, this paper proposes a distributed resource scheduling algorithm TBMADDPG based on trust model and deep reinforcement learning. Under the premise of ensuring the constraints of vehicle task unloading and resource allocation scheme, Minimize the time and energy cost consumed by the vehicle to process the task, and ensure that the vehicle in the system can complete the task calculation or unloading in a trusted environment.

© ICST Institute for Computer Sciences, Social Informatics and Telecommunications Engineering 2024
Published by Springer Nature Switzerland AG 2024. All Rights Reserved
D.-J. Deng and J.-C. Chen (Eds.): SGIoT 2023, LNICST 557, pp. 45–50, 2024.
https://doi.org/10.1007/978-3-031-55976-1_5

2 Related Works

In recent years, the global trust model analysis based on direct trust and indirect trust in the scene of vehicle networking is diverse. The distributed trust mechanism model proposed by Ke et al. comprehensively considers the information interaction between vehicles and subgrade units and the decay of trust over time and other factors [2]. The study [3] introduced timestamp mechanisms and blockchain concepts into trust management systems. Feng et al. used the satisfaction function of the service and the degradation factor function of time to improve the direct trust value described by the Bayes equation and improve the accuracy of the indirect trust model through an improved gray correlation method [4].

With the popularity of machine learning and its potential in the field of IoT applications, more and more researchers are applying this technology in the strategy optimization of task offloading and resource scheduling. For example, in the study [5, 6], LSTM algorithm is used to dynamically predict the edge communication and computing resources of mobile users, and make decisions based on the predicted future data. In the face of the challenges of vehicle computing intensive applications, multi-agent training reduces the instability in the environment and ensures that the strategy is updated [7].

3 System Model

Assumed that the intersection has two types of subgrade service units, including normal and malicious, and are connected to each other through optical fibers. To improve the model's ability to identify malicious subgrade units and balance the allocation of edge resources, this paper proposes a distributed resource scheduling algorithm TBMADDPG based on trusted model and deep reinforcement learning, so that the system can identify malicious subgrade units while reducing the overall time and energy consumption.

For all vehicles and subgrade units, the global trust matrix can be expressed as: $TrustMatrix(t) = [Trust_{i,j}(t)]$. In the description of the trust degree of the subgrade unit, the trust coefficient of the subgrade unit in a certain time slot is defined as the average of the global trust value of all vehicles, which can be expressed as: $Trust_j(t) = \sum_{i=1}^{n} Trust_{i,j}(t)/n$.

In the model, the subgrade unit to provide vehicles also dynamic change of computing resources, with the allocation rate denoted by T_R^t. The global trust matrix of the model is updated according to the interaction between the vehicle and the subgrade unit in each time slot. The vehicle's own state information is first defined as: $s_i(t) = [\tau_{max}, E_{r,j}, t_{w,j}]$. And The system state space of the current timeslot t can be defined as: $S_t = (s_1(t), s_2(t), \cdots, s_n(t), t_{w,m}, T_R^t, TrustMatrix)$.

Since all the vehicle's task is not completed by the vehicle itself is unloaded to the calculation model of a calculated in subgrade unit, so the vehicle i in current time slot t uninstall decisions can be expressed as a $(m + 1) \times 1$ matrix. So, the system dynamic space can be finally expressed as a $(m + 1) \times n$ matrix.

It can be seen that within a certain time slot in the entire model can have $(m + 1)^n$ kind action choice. As the increase of model of unit in the vehicle, the number of action space will be to exponential growth make the space is too big, so as to cause the dimension explosion. Therefore, the multi-agent algorithm is adopted to solve this problem. In the actual multi-agent environment, it is assumed that agent A can obtain the behavioral strategies of other agents and train A's own network according to the corresponding experience generated. Each agent can learn by training several different strategies and choosing a general strategy.

Suppose there are K agents in the centralized training process, and the network parameters are $\theta = \{\theta_1, \theta_2, \cdots, \theta_K\}$. The deterministic strategy of all agents can be expressed as $\mu = \{\mu_{\theta_1}, \mu_{\theta_2}, \cdots, \mu_{\theta_K}\}$. The deterministic policy μ_k for agent k is:

$$\nabla_{\theta_k} J(\mu_k) = \mathbb{E}_{S,A \sim D}\left[\nabla_{\theta_k} \mu_k(a_k|s_k)\nabla_{a_k} Q_k^\mu(S, a_1, a_2, \cdots, a_K)|_{a_k=\mu_k(s_k)}\right]$$

For Critic networks, updates can be made according to the loss function:

$$Loss(\theta_k) = \mathbb{E}_{S,A,S',R}\left[\left(Q_k^\mu(S, a_1, a_2, \cdots, a_K) - y\right)^2\right]$$

$$y = r_k + \gamma Q_k^{\mu'}(S', a_1', a_2', \cdots, a_K')|_{a_j'=\mu_j'(s_j)}$$

(1)

The Actor network can be updated by minimizing the policy gradient of the agent:

$$\nabla_{\theta_k} J \approx \frac{1}{Z}\sum_j \nabla_{\theta_k} \mu_k(s_k^j)\nabla_{a_k} Q_k^\mu(S^j, a_1^j, a_2^j, \cdots, a_K^j)|_{a_k=\mu_k(s_k^j)}$$

(2)

In order to ensure the stability of the training process, DDPG algorithm uses "soft update" to update some parameters of the target network. The update relation is (Fig. 1):

$$\theta^{Q'} \leftarrow \tau\theta^Q + (1-\tau)\theta^{Q'}$$

(3)

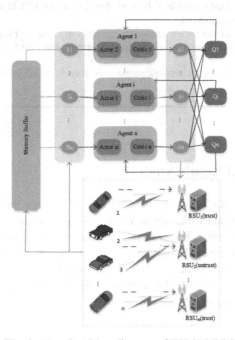

Fig. 1. The algorithm diagram of TBMADDPG

The specific training process of TBMADDPG algorithm is shown in Table 1.

Table 1. TBMADDPG training algorithm description for N agents

1	Randomly initialize all Actor and Critic networks and their respective weight parameters and their corresponding experience pools
2	Initializes information such as computing resources and network status in the system model
3	Initializing the direct and global trust matrix, and randomly specifying the malicious subgrade unit index
4	**For** episode = 1 to max_ episodes:
5	Initialize the action in the process of exploring the environment parameters: noise variable N_t subgrade unit, vehicle and information;
6	**For** time = 1 to max_ slots:
7	Randomly generate and sort vehicle task information in the current time slot.
8	Update the subgrade unit resource allocation in the model
9	**For** task = 1 to max_ indexes:
10	Each agent outputs actions based on the current policy network and noise perturbations and constraints $a_i = \mu_{\theta_i} + N_t$
11	Perform the action $a = (a_1, a_2, \cdots, a_n)$ to get rewarded r, and the next status s'
12	Waiting time delay queue updates, and the sample data (s, a, r, s') deposit pool R experience
13	**End For**
14	Calculate the global trust of all vehicles to the subgrade unit under the current time slot and update it
15	**For** agent = 1 to N:
16	Randomly sample Z bars of data (s^j, a^j, r^j, s'^j) in experience pool R to form mini batch
17	Update the online network parameters of Critic by formula (1).
18	Update the online network parameters of Actor by formula (2).
19	**End For**
20	Update the Target network parameters of each agent by formula (3)
21	**End For**
22	**End For**

4   Simulation and Result Analysis

In order to verify the validity of resource allocation strategy based on trust model in vehicle edge computing network, subgrade units are divided into normal subgrade units and malicious subgrade units. The malicious subunit not only provides false computing resources but also leaks task information, so the task should be avoided to be unloaded into the malicious subunit. In the simulation, the model randomly selects two subgrade units as malicious subgrade units. Regardless of the type of subgrade unit, all vehicles have an initial trust rating of 0.5 in them.

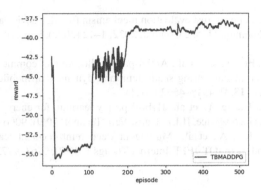

Fig. 2. Algorithm convergence curve

Figure 2 shows the training results of the TBMADDPG algorithm. As can be seen from the figure, after several fluctuations, the algorithm reaches a stable state in 400 rounds. The effect of the model increases rapidly in about 100 rounds because the multi-agent model first stores the experience group into its own experience pool during interactive learning, and then trains the network when the capacity of the experience pool is full. In fact, the model has achieved a good training effect in about 250 rounds, so the training speed of TBMADDPG algorithm is still relatively fast, and a reasonable unloading scheme with minimum delay and energy consumption based on the trust model can be obtained.

5 Future Work

In the simulation of this paper, the proposed algorithms are all based on DDPG algorithm. Considering the shortcomings of DDPG algorithm itself, other reinforcement learning algorithms, such as PPO and A3C, can be adopted in the subsequent research for simulation solutions, which may get better training results or achieve the purpose of simplifying the work.

The actions taken by the agent in this paper are actually from the direct interaction between the vehicle and the subgrade unit, and there is a "heavy unloading" situation in real life, that is, some actions need to be judged by a third party whether to continue to perform. In the face of this problem, the current reinforcement learning is difficult to learn the optimal strategy because of the selfishness of the third-party system nodes.

References

1. Chettri, L., Bera, R.: A comprehensive survey on Internet of Things (IoT) toward 5G wireless systems. IEEE Internet Things J. **7**(1), 16–32 (2020)
2. Ke, X., Zhou, G., Du, Z.: Trust evaluation model for P2P networks based on time and interaction. MATEC Web Conf. **208**, 05005 (2018)
3. El-Sayed, H., Alexander, H., Kulkarni, P., et al.: A novel multifaceted trust management framework for vehicular networks. IEEE Trans. Intell. Transp. Syst. **23**(11), 20084–20097 (2022)

4. Feng, X., Yuan, Z.: A novel trust evaluation mechanism for edge device access of the Internet of things. Wirel. Commun. Mobile Comput. **2022**, 1–12 (2022). https://doi.org/10.1155/2022/3015206
5. Rago, A., Piro, G., Boggia, G., et al.: Antici-patory allocation of communication and computational resources at the edge using spatio-temporal dynamics of mobile users. IEEE Trans. Netw. Serv. Manage. **18**(4), 4548–4562 (2021)
6. Zheng, C., Liu, S., Huang, Y., et al.: Hybrid policy learning for energy-latency trade off in MEC-assisted VR video service. IEEE Trans. Veh. Technol. **70**(9), 9006–9021 (2021)
7. Zhu, X., Luo, Y., Liu, A., et al.: Multiagent deep reinforcement learning for vehicular computation offloading in IOT. IEEE Internet Things J. **8**(12), 9763–9773 (2020)

Rule Generation for Network Intrusion Detection Systems Based on Packets-To-Video Transformation

Sheng-Tzong Cheng[✉], Yu-Ling Cheng, and Ka-Chun Cheung

National Cheng Kung University, Tainan, Taiwan
stevecheng1688@gmail.com

Abstract. Modern intrusion detection systems utilize machine learning to identify network anomalies. Traditional static rules may not be sufficient to combat
emerging attacks, making it critical to adopt a dynamic approach for keeping intrusion detection rules up-to-date. This study introduces an intelligent rule generator
with a packet encoding method to represent packets into images, a vision model to
encode the images, and a video captioning model, mapping image features to textual descriptions, thereby generating rules suitable for network intrusion detection
systems. The results of our simulated data experiments show that our classification
model has a higher accuracy than others and is capable of generating rules.

Keywords: Rule-based Network Intrusion Detection System · Rule Generator ·
Video Captioning · Network Security

1 Introduction

With the emergence of generative artificial intelligence, there has been a shift from
traditional classification problems to generating new content, such as articles and images.
This trend has also extended to network security, where past studies focused primarily
on classifying packet flow, identifying whether it is an attack or what kind of attack it
is. However, recent studies have incorporated generative artificial intelligence into this
domain.

Intrusion Detection Systems (IDS) have traditionally relied on pre-defined rules.
However, with the rapid changes in network environments and evolving intrusion techniques, pre-defined rules often need to respond more quickly to novel intrusion behaviors.
Furthermore, updating the rule set of IDS is not only time-consuming but also labor-
intensive. Therefore, integrating generative artificial intelligence into IDS can offer a
more efficient solution to adapt to the ever-changing network traffic.

By leveraging generative artificial intelligence, IDS can evolve from reactive to
proactive systems. IDS can learn from its environment, adapt to new threats, and generate

This research is supported by the project of National Science and Technology Council, Taiwan,
R.O.C under project no. NSTC 112-2218-E-006-012.

D.-J. Deng and J.-C. Chen (Eds.): SGIoT 2023, LNICST 557, pp. 51–65, 2024.
https://doi.org/10.1007/978-3-031-55976-1_6

new rules autonomously. This approach can significantly reduce the time and resources required to update the rule set of IDS.

This paper proposes an alternative approach to traditional generations. Firstly, we collect network traffic datasets containing common attacks. We convert packets into images to further process this data and build our architecture for attack classification and feature extraction from traffic data. Subsequently, we employ these features to train the captioning model, LSTM, for generating new rules for IDS.

The remaining sections of this paper are structured as follows: Sect. 2 discusses related work, including prior research and methods relevant to our study. Section 3 describes our approach regarding traffic data preprocessing, feature extractors, and captioning models. Section 4 elaborates on the specific implementation details of our experiments, including dataset collection, training processes, and evaluation metrics. Finally, we conclude our research findings and discuss future work and potential areas for improvement in Sect. 5.

2 Related Work

2.1 Problem for Problem Formulation

Our objective is to generate rules for a Network Intrusion Detection System (NIDS) based on video recognition of packet flow. Given a training dataset D, where $D = \{A_i | i$ represents the index of attack$\}$. Each attack A_i in the dataset consists of the corresponding rule R_i for the NIDS and several traffic data P_j^k, where j refers to the traffic data instance index and k represents the packet index of the traffic data P_j. The formula (1) is the structure of our data.

$$D = \{A_i | A_i = \{P_1, P_2, \ldots, P_N\}, where \, P_j = \{P_j^1, P_j^2, \ldots, P_j^m\}\} \tag{1}$$

We convert each packet P_j^k into an image representation, denoted as F_j^k. Furthermore, collecting packet images F_j as a Flow-Video can be interpreted as a traffic data flow. Our task aims to develop a function f that maps the Flow-Video F_j to the corresponding rule R_i, i.e., $R_i = f(F_j)$. This function f takes the frame representations as input and generates the NIDS rule associated with the traffic data flow.

Our task aims to develop a function f that maps the Flow-Video F_j to the corresponding rule R_i, i.e., $R_i = f(F_j)$. This function f takes the frame representations as input and generates the NIDS rule associated with the traffic data flow.

By solving this problem, we aim to provide an approach for generating NIDS rules based on packet video recognition, enabling more effective and adaptable intrusion detection in network security.

2.2 Rule Generator

T. Vollmer et al. [1] implement a Genetic Algorithm (GA) to create rules autonomously. N. Fallahi et al. [2] generated eight new features for flow-based intrusion detection. A. Sagala et al. [3] created and activated the Snort rule automatically based on the data sent by the honeypot server. Laryea et al. [4] train a neural network to generate partially effective malware rules for the Snort IPS.

2.3 Network Traffic Classification

Detecting abnormal traffic is crucial to Network Security, particularly when utilizing machine learning methods. Traffic Classification involves various techniques, but feature-based and image-based methods are two common ways to preprocess flow data. The following section will discuss the prior work on traffic classification.

Feature-Based. A flow consists of a group of packets within a time window, and the feature extractor extracts the features of the flow. Most studies used CIC-IDS2017 and CIC-IDS2018 [5] datasets with extracted features to classify whether the packets are benign or abnormal.

R. Li et al. [6] design a system that can classify a single packet without assembling IP packets into flows. M. Verkerken et al. [7] propose a novel multi-stage approach for hierarchical intrusion detection performing binary and multi-class detection, including known and zero-day attacks.

Image-Based. S. Potluri et al. [8] convert the features of the NSL-KDD dataset to a binary vector space and then represent the binaries into an 8×8 image. Identify different network attacks on ICS that mainly impact the security parameters' availability and confidentiality using CNN. H. -K. Lim et al. [9] treat the payload of packets as image data and use the convolutional neural network (CNN) and residual network (ResNet) to classify network traffic. K. Millar et al. [10] introduce flow-image representing network traffic and create a CNN model to exploit the known properties of TCP/IP packets.

2.4 Video Captioning

Video captioning generates textual descriptions for videos, conveying critical information without the need to watch. It involves analyzing video frames to extract visual features and identify objects, actions, and scenes. 3D CNN models such as C3D and R3D are commonly used for this task. These visual features are combined with language models, employing deep learning techniques like LSTM or transformers to generate accurate captions. Figure 1 illustrates the procedure of video captioning.

Visual Model. In Fig. 2 (a) C3D, D. Tran et al. [11] develop deep 3-dimensional convolutional networks (3D ConvNets) called C3D trained on a large-scale supervised video dataset. (b) R3D, Residual learning introduced skip-connected that directly connects earlier layers to the last layers. D. Tran et al. [12] proposed a 3D-convnets combined with residual learning called R3D. (c) R(2 + 1)D, in [12], the authors also proposed an architecture based on the theory that it may be more conveniently approximated by a 2D convolution followed by a 1D convolution called R(2 + 1)D.

Language Model. H. Sak et al. [13] present a recurrent neural network (RNN) type designed to capture long-term dependencies in sequential data and address the vanishing gradient problem using memory cells and gating mechanisms. LSTM can generate or predict the next word or sequence of words in a given text. The input to the LSTM language model is a sequence of words or characters, typically encoded as numerical representations.

Our problem can be seen as a video captioning task using Flow-Video as the input and the NIDS rule as the output. R. Pasunuru et al. [14] proposed a method for enhancing video captioning through multimodal, multi-task learning. They introduced temporally and logically directed knowledge into the process by incorporating video prediction and entailment generation tasks. Bairui Wang et al. [15] propose RecNet, an encoder-decoder-reconstructor architecture for video captioning. It utilizes forward and backward flows with specialized global and local structure restoration reconstructions. Wenjie Pei et al. [16] use ResNeXt-101 with 3D convolutions pretrained on the Kinetics dataset to extract 3D features and propose MARN, a Memory-Attended Recurrent Network for video captioning that utilizes a memory structure to enhance word understanding and improve captioning quality.

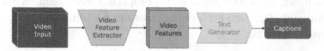

Fig. 1. Video captioning procedure

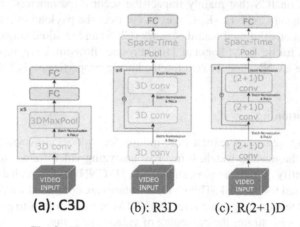

(a): C3D   (b): R3D   (c): R(2+1)D

Fig. 2. Three type of 3D CNN model architecture

3 Methods

3.1 Encoding Network Traffic

In [10], the authors investigated the representation of network traffic as square matrix pixel images, specifically analyzing byte values in network packets. They successfully classified the UNSW-NB15 dataset using CNNs, like image classification techniques. Building upon their work, the authors further improved the process [17] by employing a One-to-Multi Mapping method to encode packet byte values. Inspired by this encoding scheme, we adopted it to treat traffic data as a video. We generated 512 images based on the packets, referred to as Flow-Video.

The following steps outline the process by which the scheme encodes network traffic, as depicted in Fig. 3.

Step 1: We apply a zero mask to the digits representing destination and source IP addresses.

Step 2: We extract each packet's hexadecimal digits from the packet byte values. For instance, referring to Fig. 3, the first-byte value of the network traffic is $0 \times 5c$. We split it into "5" and "c." Utilizing base-16 hexadecimal representation, "5" can be represented by the range 0×50 to $0 \times 5F$ (i.e., 80_{10} to 95_{10}), and "c" can be represented by the range $0 \times C0$ to $0 \times CF$ (i.e., 192_{10} to 207_{10}). We then map the midpoints of the two sub-ranges, 0×58 and $0 \times C8$, to two 2×2 sub-matrices.

Step 3: All sub-matrices are combined to form a matrix representing the entire packet.

To formulate the process, let $A = a_n \dots a_1 a_0$ represent the byte value for a packet after masking the IP address, where n is the length of the packet byte value (limited to less than 1024). For the ith digit a_i, , we apply the conversion (2) to obtain b_i.

$$b_i = f_c(a_i) = (a_i \times 16) + (16/2) \tag{2}$$

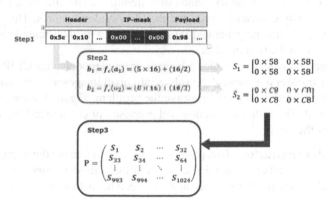

Fig. 3. Packet encoding procedure

After the conversion using f_c, A is transformed into B. We then repeat b_i to create a 2×2 sub-matrix:

$$S_i = [[b_i, b_i], [b_i, b_i]] \tag{3}$$

The matrix P is constructed as a 64×64 matrix comprising the sub-matrices S_i in (3):

$$P[s+2 : s+4, t : t+2] = S_i \tag{4}$$

where $s = i/64$ and $t = i \bmod 64$

For a network traffic flow $P_j = P_j^k$, we convert each packet P_j^k in P_j into a matrix using the abovementioned encoding. Consequently, we perceive a network traffic flow F_j, as a Flow-Video composed of several packet images, which will serve as the input for our subsequent model.

3.2 Architecture

We aim to generate one rule R = $\{w_1, w_2, \ldots, w_n\}$, where w_i represent the word of the rule to describe the given malicious packet flow F. To address the problem, we employ an encoder-decoder mechanism, where the encoder extracts the features of flow-video frames, and the decoder generates the IDS rule with frame features as input. The distribution of the output rule word $\{w_1, w_2, \ldots, w_{|R|}\}$ corresponding to the input:

$$P(R|F) = P(w_1, w_2, \ldots, w_{|R|}|F) = \prod_i P(w_i|w_{<i}, F; \theta) \tag{5}$$

where θ denotes the parameters of the encoder-decoder model, $|R|$ denotes the length of the words in the rule, $w_{(<i)}$ means the previous generated words (i.e., $\{w_1, w_2, \ldots, w_{(i-1)}\}$).

Equation (5) quantifies the likelihood of generating a specific word given the context of the previously generated words and the Flow-Video features. This probabilistic formulation ensures that the generated IDS rule aligns with the semantic and syntactic patterns observed in the training data.

Most image-text matching studies rely on pretrained models, like CLIP [18]. Unlike the studies, we transfer our packet byte values into pixel images as input. As a result, we can't just apply a pretrained model to solve the problem. Figure 4 shows the architecture we proposed. The following section will propose our customized encoder-decoder mechanism for the input.

Encoder: Feature Extractor. To caption well, we need to find out the important features of our flow-video. Unlike the studies using pretrained models, since we transfer our packet byte values into pixel images as input, we need to customize and train the encoder

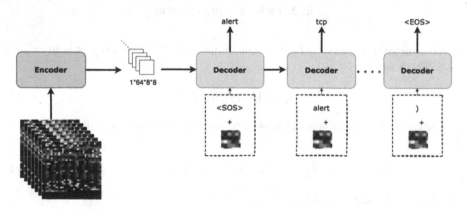

Fig. 4. Proposed **architecture**

ourselves. Consider the flow-video is a 3D-data, and use 3D-CNNs models, C3D, R3D, and R(2 + 1)D [11, 12], as our baseline model. Further, we reconstructed the 3D-CNNs model, called "PAC3D", to be more compatible with our pixel images input.

(2 + 1)D conv Block. To capture every packet information's temporal feature, we first employ spatial convolution to capture every packet's spatial feature:

$$Conv_{spatial} = y[i, j, k] = \sum_{n} \sum_{l} x[i, j - n, k - l] \cdot h[1, n, l] \tag{6}$$

where x represents input, y represents output, h represents kernel, i, j, k represent the position of the output element, and n, l represent offset within the kernel.

After obtaining spatial features, we do the temporal convolution to get the temporal correlation of these spatial features:

$$Conv_{temporal} = y[i, j, k] = \sum_{m} x[i - m, j, k] \cdot h[m, 1, 1] \tag{7}$$

where x represents input, y represents output, h represents kernel, i, j, k represent the position of the output element, and m represents offset within the kernel.

The (2 + 1)D conv block is the orange one shown in Fig. 5, and the formulation equation is following:

$$Conv_{2Plus1D} = Conv_{temporal}(Conv_{spatial}(x)) \tag{8}$$

Residual Block. The blue block in Fig. 5 represents the residual block, which introduces the residual network concept:

$$y = Conv(Conv(x)) + x \tag{9}$$

where x is the input of the residual block, and y is the output of the residual block.

3D Conv Block.

$$Conv_{3D} = y[i, j, k] = \sum_{m} \sum_{n} \sum_{l} x[i - m, j - n, k - l] \cdot h[m, n, l] \tag{10}$$

where x represents input, y represents output, h represents kernel, i, j, k represent the position of the output element, and m, n, l represent offset within the kernel.

After the convolutions, we performed global average pooling over the whole volume. And the output of our model is the classification result of the Flow-Video. Remove the fully connected layer; the result is the input of the language model introduced in the following paragraph.

Decoder: Language Generator. With the features of flow-video, we combine it with the rule word sequence as our decoder output. We use the LSTM network as our language model to generate the captions with its ability to maintain long-term dependencies. (11)–(16) show the LSTM operation.

$$f_s = \sigma\left(W_f[h_{s-1}, x_s] + b_f\right) \tag{11}$$

$$i_s = \sigma\left(W_i[h_{s-1}, x_s] + b_i\right) \tag{12}$$

$$o_s = \sigma\left(W_o[h_{s-1}, x_s] + b_o\right) \tag{13}$$

$$\widetilde{c}_s = tanh\left(W_c[h_{s-1}, x_s] + b_c\right) \tag{14}$$

$$c_s = f_s * c_{s-1} + i_s * \widetilde{c}_s \tag{15}$$

$$h_s = o_t * tanh(c_s) \tag{16}$$

where f_s represents forget gate, i_s represents input gate, o_s represents output gate, h_s represents the hidden state, h_{s-1} represents the output of previous cell, c_t represents cell gate, $\widetilde{c}_s$ represents the candidate for cell gate, W_g, b_g represent the weight and bias of respective gate g, x_s refers to the input of current step, and σ refers to sigmoid function. Figure 6 shows the LSTM cell.

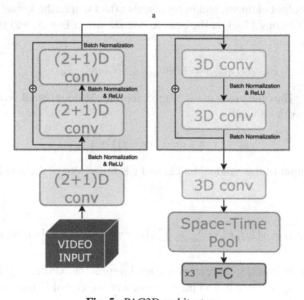

Fig. 5. PAC3D architecture

4   Implementation and Experiments

4.1   Dataset

Despite several existing datasets for IDS, such as CIC-IDS2017, CIC-IDS2018 [5], UNSW-15 [19], and NSL-KDD [20], these datasets lack sufficient information for conducting a comprehensive analysis of the task. One limitation is the absence of original packet capture (PCAP) data. In contrast, another limitation is the lack of specific attack time information, making identifying the range of attack packets challenging. Consequently, we collected data, which involved capturing real-world PCAPs containing four different attacks and benign data. We used Wireshark, a packet capture tool, to collect the dataset to capture the network's packet flow. We set two VM, one with Kali Linux as the attacker OS and another with BeeBox (a custom Linux VM pre-installed with bWAPP) as the victim OS. Figure 7 illustrates the network structure of our environment. The data collection period lasts four days, starting from 17:00 on Wednesday, April 26, 2023, and concluding at 23:40 on Saturday, April 29, 2023. The implemented attacks included Brute Force SSH using Patator, DoS Goldeneye, DDoS LOIC, Heartbleed, and PortScan. For each attack category, we conducted the attack almost 200 times. Table 1 shows the records of times and numbers of attacks. Before each simulated attack, we captured normal traffic data for 1 min and continued capturing for an additional 1 min after the attack concluded. To streamline the data collection process, we developed scripts to automate the execution of the attacks and configured Wireshark to save the captured data at the designated times.

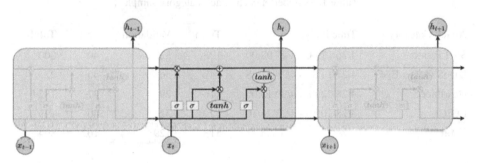

Fig. 6. LSTM cell

4.2 Implementation Details

Training Environment. We use a computer with NVIDIA GeForce RTX 3090 to train our models. Table 2 provides detailed information about our experimental environment.

Training Procedure and Evaluate Metrics. We train our model in two stages since we can't use a pretrained model and must train the feature extractor by ourselves.

Stage 1. Feature Extractor. We train our feature extractor as an attack type classifier using our dataset with the Flow-Video as input and the attack type as output. We employ Adam [21] gradient descent optimization to optimize our loss function Cross Entropy Loss (17) and perform training for 30 epochs with a learning rate decayed by 0.1 every ten epochs.

$$H(p, q) = -\Sigma_x(p(x) \log q(x)) \tag{17}$$

where p(x) is our predicted attack type and q(x) is the actual attack type when x is input.

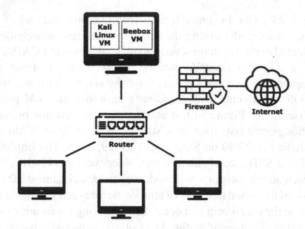

Fig. 7. The network structure of our environment.

Table 1. Number of each attack category sample

Attack Category	Time Range	Train	Validation	Test	**Total**
SSH Patator	4/26 17:00 - 4/27 08:00	128	32	40	200
DDoS GoldenEye	4/27 14:38 - 4/28 07:38	142	36	45	223
Heartbleed	4/28 22:48 - 4/29 15:00	116	29	37	182
LOIC	4/28 10:10 - 4/28 20:10	127	32	40	199
Total		513	129	162	804

Table 2. Experimental environment settings

Item	Setting
OS	Ubuntu 20.04.4 LTS
Program language	Python 3.7.16
CUDA/ cuDNN	11.6 / 8.2.1
TensorFlow	2.8.0
CPU	AMD Ryzen 9 5950X 16-Core Processor
GPU	NVIDIA GeForce RTX 3090
RAM	32GB

To evaluate our model, we use accuracy, precision, recall, and F1 with confusion matrixes to calculate and analyze.

$$Accuracy = \frac{|CorrectPredictions|}{|TotalPrediction|} \tag{18}$$

$$Precision = \frac{TruePositives}{TruePositives + FalsePositives} \tag{19}$$

$$Recall = \frac{TruePositives}{TruePositives + FalseNegatives} \tag{20}$$

$$F1 = \frac{2 \times Precision \times Recall}{Precision + Recall} \tag{21}$$

where all the metrics are as higher as possible.

Stage 2. Language Model. We use the pretrained model in Stage 1 and train our language model with Cross Entropy Loss as the loss function and Adam gradient descent as the optimizer. Perform training for 30 epochs with LSTM hidden size set as 256 and the word embedding size set as 256. After each LSTM layer in our language model, we applied dropout regularization with a probability of 0.5.

We employ two standard evaluation metrics in a captioning task to evaluate our language model. The following y denotes the actual word and y/ denotes the predicted word:

$$ROUGE_L = F_{LCS} = \frac{(1+\beta^2)R_{LCS}P_{LCS}}{R_{LCS}+\beta^2 P_{LCS}} \tag{22}$$

where $P_{LCS} = \frac{\text{LCS}(y,y')}{\text{len}(y)}$, $R_{LCS} = \frac{\text{LCS}(y,y')}{\text{len}(y')}$, LCS represents least common multiple.

$$BLEU = BP \times exp\left(\sum_{n=1}^{N} W_n \times \log P_n\right) \tag{23}$$

where $BP = \min\left(1, \exp\left(1 - \frac{actuallength}{gerneatedlength}\right)\right)$, W_n represent the weight and $P_n = \frac{\{number\ of\ n-gram\ matches\}}{\{number\ of\ total\ n_{grams}\ in\ gerneated\ output\}}$.

4.3 Experiments and Discussion

During our experiment, we examined input data sizes as 512 packets to generate captions for the resulting rules. Initially, we compared the performance of our feature extractor "PAC3D" as a classification model to baseline models C3D, R3D, and R(2 + 1)D. Additionally, we evaluated their performance when paired with the same language model. The accuracy results presented are an average performance from ten training runs. And the other metrics show the best model performance.

Classification Model. Table 3 shows the results of testing the baseline model: C3D, R3D, and R(2 + 1)D on our dataset. From the result, we can observe that our model "PAC3D" have higher accuracy than the other three models. However, accuracy may not be the only evaluation we should consider. We also value the trade-off of precision and recall, where are average scores of each class. Our model also has the most balance between Precision and Recall. Figure 8 indicates the confusion matrixes of the four models with the highest accuracy in each ever tested. A comparison of the four results reveals that our model can averagely classify the attack categories well.

Table 3. The results of attack classification model (encoder)

Model Name	Accuracy	Precision	Recall	F1
C3D	0.24	0.21	0.26	0.23
R3D	0.58	0.63	0.60	0.62
R(2 + 1)D	0.64	0.60	0.68	0.64
PAC3D(proposed)	**0.76**	**0.80**	**0.80**	**0.8**

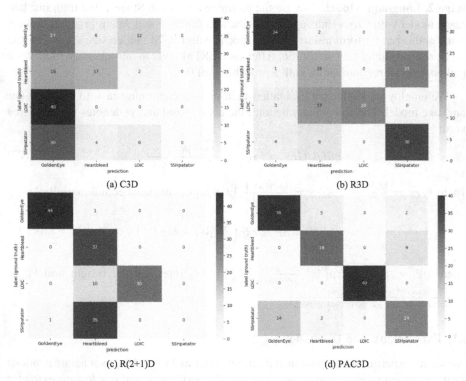

(a) C3D

(b) R3D

(c) R(2+1)D

(d) PAC3D

Fig. 8. The confusion matrixes (a) C3D (b) R3D (c) R(2 + 1)D (d) PAC3D

Captioning. In Table 4, we can observe that our model demonstrates superior captioning performance based on both evaluation metrics. However, it is important to note that the BLEU@1 scores appear to be relatively low for all models. This is primarily because the BLEU@1 metric is designed to measure similarity between short and simple sentences, whereas our objective is to generate complex and machine-readable network intrusion detection system rules. Therefore, the low BLEU@1 scores do not necessarily indicate poor performance in our specific task. Instead, they reflect the inherent challenges of evaluating rule-based captions, which tend to be longer and less human-readable.

Table 4. The results of captioning model with different classifiers

Model Name	BLEU@1	ROUGE
C3D + LSTM	\	\
R3D + LSTM	0.13	0.61
R(2 + 1)D + LSTM	0.13	0.77
PAC3D + LSTM (proposed)	0.11	0.89

Furthermore, in Table 5, we present a comparison between the target rules and the generated rules. The results indicate that the generated rules align perfectly with the target rules, providing evidence that our model captures the desired correlations effectively. However, this also suggests that our dataset might be too small for the captioning task, as the generator can easily capture the word correlations within the limited data.

Table 5. The comparison of the target rules and the generated rules

Target rules	Generated rules
alert tcp $EXTERNAL_NET any - > $HOME_NET any (msg:"ET DOS Inbound Low Orbit Ion Cannon LOIC DDOS Tool desu string"; flow:to_server,established; content:"desudesudesu"; nocase; threshold: type limit,track by_src,seconds 180,count 1; reference:url,www.isc.sans. org/diary.html?storyid=10051; classtype:trojan-activity; sid:2012049; rev:5; metadata:created_at 2010_12_13, updated_at 2010_12_13;)	alert tcp $EXTERNAL_NET any - > $HOME_NET any (msg:"ET DOS Inbound Low Orbit Ion Cannon LOIC DDOS Tool desu string"; flow:to_server,established; content:"desudesudesu"; nocase; threshold: type limit,track by_src,seconds 180,count 1; reference:url,www.isc.sans. org/diary.html?storyid=10051; classtype:trojan-activity; sid:2012049; rev:5; metadata:created_at 2010_12_13, updated_at 2010_12_13;)
alert tcp $EXTERNAL_NET any - > $HOME_NET 22 (msg:"ET SCAN Potential SSH Scan"; flow:to_server; flags:S,12; threshold: type both, track by_src, count 5, seconds 120; reference:url,en.wikipedia.org/wiki/Brute_force_attack; reference:url,doc.emergingthreats.net/2001219; classtype:attempted-recon; sid:2001219; rev:20; metadata:created_at 2010_07_30, updated_at 2010_07_30;)	alert tcp $EXTERNAL_NET any - > $HOME_NET 22 (msg:"ET SCAN Potential SSH Scan"; flow:to_server; flags:S,12; threshold: type both, track by_src, count 5, seconds 120; reference:url,en.wikipedia.org/wiki/Brute_force_attack; reference:url,doc.emergingthreats.net/2001219; classtype:attempted-recon; sid:2001219; rev:20;metadata:created_at 2010_07_30, updated_at 2010_07_30;)

5 Conclusions and Future Work

We employed a method to transform packet information into a video format and devised an architecture for generating rule captions for the network intrusion detection system using video-captioning techniques. Our proposed model incorporates spatial-temporal and comprehensive information in the encoder component, resulting in superior performance for our specific use case. Furthermore, we conducted a comparative analysis with a commonly used video captioning model to highlight the advantages of our approach.

To evaluate our model, we created a dataset by simulating various attack scenarios and performed experiments using this dataset. The results presented in Sect. 4.3 demonstrate that our model outperforms C3D, R3D, and R(2 + 1)D models in terms of performance on our dataset.

Unlike other captioning models that benefit from large pretraining datasets and can handle multiple tasks such as QA, translation, and captioning for unseen classes, our architecture has limitations due to using a smaller dataset. However, we believe that with the collection of a larger dataset, our model can excel in identifying zero-day attacks and generating network intrusion detection system rules specifically tailored to those attacks. By expanding the dataset, our model will have the potential to overcome its cur-rent limitations and achieve improved performance in capturing and addressing new and emerging security threats.

References

1. Vollmer, T., et al.: Autonomous rule creation for intrusion detection. Proc. IEEE Symposium on Computational Intelligence in Cyber Security (CICS) **2011**, 1–8 (2011)
2. Fallahi, N., et al.: Automated flow-based rule generation for network intrusion detection systems. In: Proc. 2016 24th Iranian Conference on Electrical Engineering (ICEE), pp. 1948–1953 (2016)
3. Sagala, A.: Automatic SNORT IDS rule generation based on honeypot log. In: Proc. 2015 7th International Conference on Information Technology and Electrical Engineering (ICITEE), pp. 576–580 (2015)
4. Laryea, E.N.A.: Snort Rule Generation for Malware Detection using the GPT2 Transformer. Université d'Ottawa/University of Ottawa (2022)
5. Sharafaldin, I., et al.: Toward Generating a New Intrusion Detection Dataset and Intrusion Traffic Characterization (2018)
6. Li, R., et al.: Byte Segment Neural Network for Network Traffic Classification. In: Proc. 2018 IEEE/ACM 26th International Symposium on Quality of Service (IWQoS), pp. 1–10 (2018)
7. Verkerken, M., et al.: A novel multi-stage approach for hierarchical intrusion detection. IEEE Trans. Netw. Serv. Manage. **20**(3), 3915–3929 (2023). https://doi.org/10.1109/tnsm.2023.325 9474
8. Potluri, S., et al.: Convolutional Neural Networks for Multi-class Intrusion Detection System, pp. 225–238. Springer International Publishing (2018)
9. Lim, H.-K., et al.: Packet-based network traffic classification using deep learning. In: Proc. 2019 International Conference on Artificial Intelligence in Information and Communication (ICAIIC), IEEE, pp. 046–051 (2019)
10. Millar, K., et al.: Using convolutional neural networks for classifying malicious network traffic. In: Alazab, M., Tang, M. (eds.) Deep Learning Applications for Cyber Security, pp. 103–126. Springer International Publishing (2019)
11. Tran, D., et al.: Learning Spatiotemporal Features with 3D Convolutional Networks. Proc. IEEE International Conference on Computer Vision (ICCV) **2015**, 4489–4497 (2015)
12. Tran, D., et al.: A closer look at spatiotemporal convolutions for action recognition. Proc. IEEE/CVF Conference on Computer Vision and Pattern Recognition **2018**, 6450–6459 (2018)
13. Sak, H., et al.: Long short-term memory recurrent neural network architectures for large scale acoustic modeling (2014)
14. Pasunuru, R., Bansal, M.: Multi-task video captioning with video and entailment generation. arXiv preprint arXiv:1704.07489 (2017). https://doi.org/10.48550/arXiv.1704.07489
15. Wang, B., et al.: Reconstruction Network for Video Captioning. Proc. IEEE/CVF Conference on Computer Vision and Pattern Recognition **2018**, 7622–7631 (2018)

16. Pei, W., et al.: Memory-Attended Recurrent Network for Video Captioning. Proc. IEEE/CVF Conference on Computer Vision and Pattern Recognition (CVPR) **2019**, 8339–8348 (2019)
17. Cheng, A.: PAC-GAN: Packet Generation of Network Traffic using Generative Adversarial Networks. In: Proc. 2019 IEEE 10th Annual Information Technology, Electronics and Mobile Communication Conference (IEMCON), pp. 0728-0734 (2019)
18. Radford, A., et al.: Learning transferable visual models from natural language supervision. In: Proc. International conference on machine learning, pp. 8748–8763. PMLR (2021)
19. Moustafa, N., Slay, J.: UNSW-NB15: a comprehensive data set for network intrusion detection systems (UNSW-NB15 network data set). Proc. Military Communications and Information Systems Conference (MilCIS) **2015**, 1–6 (2015)
20. Tavallaee, M., et al.: A detailed analysis of the KDD CUP 99 data set. Proc. IEEE Symposium on Computational Intelligence for Security and Defense Applications **2009**, 1–6 (2009)
21. Kingma, D.P., Ba, J.: Adam: A method for stochastic optimization. arXiv preprint arXiv: 1412.6980 (2014). https://doi.org/10.48550/arXiv.1412.6980

WLAN, Wireless Internet and 5G

Enhancing UORA for IEEE802.11be

Leu Fang Yi[✉] and Chang Chia Wen

Tunghai University, Taichung, Taiwan
leufy@thu.edu.tw

Abstract. Currently, wireless networks have been tools commonly used in our daily lives. Users frequently connect multiple devices, especially IoT devices, to wireless networks to enjoy network services, no matter whether they are at home, in libraries, or in coffee shops. Also, different kinds of real-time applications which increase huge demands of high-speed transmission have been proposed. But, these applications pose challenges to the real-time transmission performance of wireless networks. To address these issues, IEEE 802.11be incorporates the Uplink OFDMA Random Access transmission method previously developed for by IEEE 802.11ax. However, when a large number of users need to transmit data, UORA suffers from long transmission delays and low transmission throughputs, which fail to meet the requirements of real-time applications. To fulfill the low-latency demands of real-time applications, this research proposes a transmission mechanism, named Priority-based OCW (POCW for short), to adjust the OCW range for IEEE802.11be stations based on priorities of data streams. This mechanism allows higher-priority STAs to transmit data before lower-priority STAs. Our simulations show that the POCW offers lower transmission delays for time-sensitive data streams and provides better throughputs in densely populated STA environments.

Keywords: IEEE 802.11be · UORA · RTA

1 Introduction

In recent years, due to rapid advancements of wireless technology, the unprecedented demands for real-time applications (RTAs) [1] have been dramatically increased. These applications as an integral part of our modern lives include diverse domains, such as online meetings [2], multimedia streaming [3], remote education [4], and smart homes [5]. To address the increasing demand of these applications, the IEEE 802.11be Task Group (TGbe) has introduced an innovative wireless network technology, called IEEE 802.11be (Wi-Fi 7), also named Extreme High Throughput (EHT) wireless communication, which provides wireless network services required by users and ensures low latency, fast transmission speed, and high throughputs of data transmission.

In fact, IEEE 802.11ax (also known as Wi-Fi 6) [6] introduced the Uplink OFDMA Random Access (UORA) technology [7], allowing multiple users to

© ICST Institute for Computer Sciences, Social Informatics and Telecommunications Engineering 2024
Published by Springer Nature Switzerland AG 2024. All Rights Reserved
D.-J. Deng and J.-C. Chen (Eds.): SGIoT 2023, LNICST 557, pp. 69–82, 2024.
https://doi.org/10.1007/978-3-031-55976-1_7

access the network simultaneously and transmit uplink data efficiently. Besides the improvements, as the number of users grew, UORA encountered a new problem, i.e., high data transmission collision, which conducts to significant network delays. However, the latest IEEE 802.11be draft continues to incorporate UORA technology [8].

To support real-time sensitive network applications for the IEEE802.11be standard on UORA, in this study, we propose a novel data-transmission control scheme called Priority-based OCW (POCW for short). The primary objectives are twofold: Prioritize different data streams based on their respective categories, especially focusing on highly time-sensitive streams. Enhance the utilization of transmission opportunities by reducing the number of idle RUs, thereby enhancing the overall Quality of Service (QoS) of a wireless network.

The purposes are improvement of resource allocation efficiency, reduction of collision probabilities during data transmission, and the provision of efficient and reliable transmission services, particularly in a dense-user environment. Our previous research results can be found in [9].

The article is organized as follows. Section 2 presents the UORA transmission mechanism and explore the factors contributing to its suboptimal network performance. Section 3 analyzes performance of the existing UORA schemes. Section 4 explains the practice and structure of POCW. The simulations of the POCW and their results are, respectively, evaluated and discussed in Sect. 5. Section 6 concludes this study and addresses our future studies.

2 UORA and Related Studies

2.1 UORA Operations

The working principles of the UORA mechanism are as follows. During a UORA transmission opportunity (TXOP) [10], the AP initially broadcasts a Trigger Frame (TF) to all the STAs in the network. The TF conveys essential channel information, such as the number of available RUs, the size of the OFDMA contention window (OCW) [11], and the association identifiers (AIDs) [12] of the STAs eligible to contend for the RUs. Upon receiving the TF, an STA intending to transmit data starts its backoff mechanism. The AP configures the OCW size, i.e.,, which is carried in TF sent to STAs. The and, used by STAi either for an initial transmission or successful transmission (retransmission), are calculated based on Eqs. (1) and (2) [13]:

$$OCW_{min}^i = 2^{EOCW_{min}} - 1 \tag{1}$$

$$OCW_{max}^i = 2^{EOCW_{max}} - 1 \tag{2}$$

in which $1 \leq i \leq n$, where n is the number STAs now under the concerned AP; $EOCW$ standing for Extended OFDMA Contention Window is specified by two parameters: $EOCW_{min}$ and $EOCW_{max}$, which as a part of the Random Access Parameter Set (RAPS) elements [14] presented in the TF, respectively, define the lower and upper bounds of the extended contention window range that the STAs must follow. $EOCW$ is utilized to dynamically increase the OCW size to adjust the backoff stage when needed, i.e., when there is a collision on an RU, then the OCW of concerned STA, e.g., STA_i will be enlarged to reduce the probability of the following data-transmission collision. If STA_i does not receive TF from AP, the default value of are set to 7 and 31, respectively.

When a STA intends to contend for RUs, it initiates the backoff process by randomly selecting a value from the range, shown in Eq. (3):

$$initialOBO = [0, OCW_{min}] \tag{3}$$

This value then serves as the initial OFDMA backoff counter (OBO) [15]. Upon receiving the TF, the STA decreases the OBO following Eq. (4):

$$OBO = OBO - (number of available) \tag{4}$$

in which the item in the parenthesis is the number of available RU conveyed in underlying TF.

When the backoff stage ends, STA has three situations, i.e., no transmission, successful transmission, and transmission failure. The first situation is the case in which $OBO > 0$. Then, this STA must wait for its $OBO \leq 0$ in the following TXOPs. The second situation occurs, when the STA's $OBO \leq 0$. STA randomly selects an RU and successfully transmits data without collision. After that, the STA re-selects a new OBO value from the same $(0, OCW_{min})$ for the next TXOP, i.e., if the initial transmission is successful, the next OCW range is still from $(0, OCW_{min})$. But when the STA's $OBO \leq 0$, and collision occurs on data transmission, this is the third case in which new $OCW_{new} = min(2 * OCW_{min}, OCW_{max})$ and the STA randomly select a new OBO from the new OCW range, i.e., $(0, OCW_{new})$, for the next TXOP.

After the data transmission phase, the AP sends Multi-User Block Acknowledgment (MU-BACK) frames [16] as a confirmation of successful data transmission to those STAs successfully transmitting their data. On the other hand, STAs that fail to receive MU-BACK (maybe due to transmission error or fail to receive MU-BACK) will renew their OCW values, with the method described above and continue its backoff to wait for the next TXOP. The UORA process is represented in Fig. 1.

3   Related Studies

In the IEEE 802.11ax standard, the transmission efficiency of the UORA mechanism is only 37% [18] which can be attributed to two factors. First, when multiple STAs choose the same RU, collisions occur on that RU. Second, during data transmission, some RUs remain idle due to without being chosen by any STA for transmission.

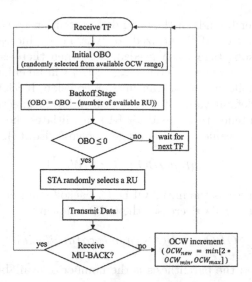

Fig. 1. The UORA Process.

To enhance the transmission efficiency of UORA, research results have been proposed [18–21]. Lanante *et al.* [19] employed a two-dimensional Markov-chain model to analyze the transmission efficiencies and throughputs of various numbers of STAs in the UORA mechanism.

Lee [20] proposed a trigger frame and the carrier sensing-based H-UORA (Hybrid Uplink OFDMA Random Access) mechanism, which incorporates a two-stage OBO backoff mechanism. Next, each STA generates a random number X_u. If $X_u < \rho_u$, the STA senses the channels where ρ_u is the OBO probability. When there are n idle channels (i.e., idle RUs), $n \geq 1$, the STA randomly selects one to transmit data. If $X_u \geq \rho_u$, the STA waits for the next round of backoff, called the second backoff. The approach enables idle RUs to have a chance of being selected by STAs during the second backoff, thereby reducing the number of idle RUs and increasing the overall transmission efficiencies and throughputs.

Kim *et al.* [18] proposed a Collision Reduction and Utilization Improvement (CRUI) mechanism to address data-transmission collisions on RUs by Extra Backoff Stage (EBO) and Opportunistic RU Hopping (ORH). The CRUI enhancements aim to improve fairness for STAs needing to transmit data by providing a second chance for STAs, aiming to select, i.e., hopping to, another RU to avoid collisions. Further, the CRUI follows the IEEE 802.11ax rule of simultaneous start of data transmission and end of transmission. However, the EBO stage occupies transmission time, and the ORH increases the possibility of transmission collisions due to hopping.

Kim *et al.* [21] introduced a solution to enhance the IEEE 802.11ax standard by conducting control over the STA's OBO counter. Instead of using a fixed OBO value, each STA dynamically determines an OBO value based on the case whether its previous transmission succeeds or not. By controlling the OBO counter, the UORA mechanism can intelligently select a suitable OBO value based on each STA's transmission status. This approach indirectly influences the likelihood of RU collisions and the availability of free-time slots for data transmissions. For instance, when a small number of STAs competing for RUs, the OBO control allows STAs to produce smaller OBO values, making them easier to successfully compete for RUs. However, when the number of competing STAs increases, the potential collisions still exist.

To face this challenge, the POCW classifies the data streams to support delay-sensitive [17] and high-data-flow applications, such as voice and video, particularly for 5G/6G network uRLLC (ultra-Reliable Low Latency communication), thus improving the overall network performance. Besides, it minimizes data-transmission collisions, and improves throughput in a dense-user environment.

4 Proposed Scheme

In this study, we use the IEEE802.11e's data classification method to divide data streams into two types, including delay-sensitive data and delay-insensitive data. The former (latter) consists of AC_VO and AC_VI (AC_BE and AC_BK).

4.1 OBO Range

In this research, as receiving $EOCW_{min}$ and $EOCW_{max}$ carried in TF, we calculate OCW_{min} and OCW_{max} by using Eqs.(1) and (2), respectively. STA's OBO value is chosen from the range $[x, OCW]$ where represents the lower limit of the OCW size for a specific TXOP, i.e., the STA randomly selects an OBO value from $[0, OCW_{min}]$ for its initial selection, where, i.e., $x = 0$ and $OCW = OCW_{min}$. After a TXOP, STAs that did not obtain a transmission opportunity, i.e., $OBO > 0$, will wait for the next TXOP. STAs that successfully transmit their data will choose a new OBO value from the same $[x, OCW]$ range without changing the values of x and OCW. A STA that does not transmit data successfully will double its OCW, and the new OBO will be randomly chosen from a revised new range as indicated in Eq. (5):

$$[x, OCW] = [X_{new}, OCW_{new}] \tag{5}$$

where $X_{new} = OCW$ and $OCW_{new} = min[OCW * 2, OCW_{max}]$. Then, STA's OBO is selected from the new range $[X, OCW]$ in order to reduce the chance of STA collisions and improve data-stream priority.

4.2 Trigger Based Multi-Carrier CSMA

In this study, we utilize a function of the TB-MC-CSMA (Trigger Based Multi-Carrier CSMA) method [28], i.e., RU granular carrier sensing, to detect idle RUs during RU sensing (RS) slot time (see Fig. 2.) to reduce the number of idle RUs in underlying TXOPs. After backoff, STA 1's $OBO = 0$. It randomly selects RU 1 to transmit data. In the general UORA mechanism, STA 2 as its $OBO = 1$ must wait for the next TXOP. But after RU sensing, RU 2 will be found to be idle. Then STA 2 backs off again. Now, $OBO = 0$. STA 2 dynamically selects RU 2 to transmit data. Thus, the probability with which RU 2 is idle in this TXOP is lowered. https://www.overleaf.com/project/64daff6c4751f2b81202dba1

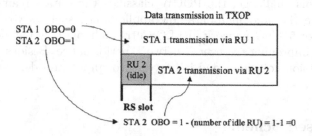

Fig. 2. TB-MC-CSMA architecture.

5   Simulations and Analyses

In this study, we simulated a BSS (Basic Service Set) [32] environment, including one AP and multiple STAs. Table 1 lists the experimental parameters. In addition, three schemes, including the UORA, H-UORA, and POCW without RS are also evaluated and compared with the POCW. POCW without RS is also known as POCW without RU sensing.

Table 1. Our experimental Parameters.

Paremeter	Value
Number of subcarrier per RU	26 tones
Number of STA	1–100
Packet Size	100/2k/10k bytes
TF duration	100 μs
SIFS duration	16 μs
PIFS duration	25 μs
MU-BACK duration	68 μs

In the following, a total of 3 experiments was performed. The first studied the throughputs and delays of the POCW. The former is defined as the number of bytes received per second at the receiving end, while delay is defined as the time that a packet travels from its sender to receiver. The second, and the third experiments were done by giving different numbers of RUs, packet sizes and bandwidths of an RU, respectively. Success probabilities, defined as the probabilities that a STA can successfully transmit its data in underlying TXOP, are also evaluated in these three experiments.

5.1 Experiment on Different Numbers of STAs for the POCW

The first experiment studied the POCW given 9 RUs and different numbers of STAs ranging from 1 to 60.

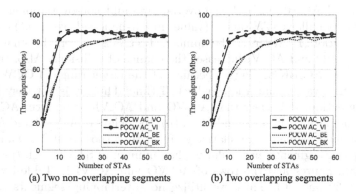

(a) Two non-overlapping segments   (b) Two overlapping segments

Fig. 3. Throughputs of the POCW on two overlapping and non-overlapping segments given 9 RUs and different numbers of STAs ranging from 1 to 60.

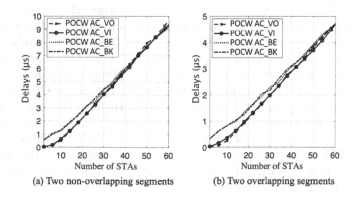

(a) Two non-overlapping segments   (b) Two overlapping segments

Fig. 4. Delays of the POCW on two overlapping and non-overlapping segments given 9 RUs and different numbers of STAs ranging from 1 to 60.

Figure 3 and 4 present throughputs and delays of the POCW, respectively. Figure 3 illustrates that when numbers of STAs are lower, throughputs of AC_VO and AC_VI are higher than those of AC_BE and AC_BK, no matter whether it is an overlapping or non-overlapping segment. This is because, when the number of STAs and the OCW range are both small, STAs that would like to deliver AC_VO or AC_VI have higher opportunities to transmit due to generating smaller OBO values (higher probabilities) to win contention. The system throughputs are saturated (see Fig. 3.) at 9 RUs because only 9 RUs are available. However, as the number of STAs increases, the throughputs of the non-overlapping-segments are not higher than those of the overlapping-segments. This is because the small OCW range of non-overlapping segments increases the probabilities of transmission collisions, which in turn leads to a decrease of throughputs.

Figure 4 illustrates that the delays of AC_VO and AC_VI are lower than those of AC_BE and AC_BK in both the overlapping and non-overlapping segments because their smaller OCW ranges (values in left-hand-side segment) contribute to win contention. However, as the number of STAs is higher, the smaller OCW range of AC_VO and AC_VI increases the chance of collisions. Also, the delays of AC_BE and AC_BK are longer because of the larger range of OCW, leading to bigger OBO values and a longer backoff time. Thus, it is not easy for them to win contention. It is clear that AC_VO and AC_VI outperform AC_BE and AC_BK. Comparing Fig. 4.(a) and Fig. 4.(b), the delays of AC_VO and AC_VI on non-overlapping segments are relatively higher than those of AC_VO and AC_VI on overlapping segments, particularly when number of STA is high (please refer to these two figures and the rows of AC_VO and AC_VI in Table 4 when No. of STAs is 30 and 50). Thus, we utilize non-overlapping segments to do the following experiments.

5.2   Experiment on Different RUs

The second experiment was performed on different numbers of RUs, including 9, 18, 37 RUs. Figure 5, 6 and 7, respectively, illustrate the throughputs, success probabilities and delays of the four tested schemes. As shown in Fig. 5., the UORA exhibits the lowest throughputs regardless of the number of RUs, meaning that its function can be further enhanced. On 9 RUs and 18 STAs, the H-UORA achieves the highest throughputs of 86Mbps, surpassing the POCW by about 5Mbps. This is because in the POCW, the larger OCW of AC_BE and AC_BK results in lower throughputs due to the fact that their OBOs are often (not usually) larger than those of AC_VO and AC_VI. As the number of STAs increases, throughputs of the H-UORA are lower than those of the POCW because POCW optimizes the OCW range, thus maintaining its throughputs. If we check the Y-axes of Fig. 5.(a), 5.(b) and 5.(c), we can see that the throughputs of the 4 test schemes on 37 RUs at any specific number of STA, e.g., k STAs, $10 \leq k \leq 100$, almost individually double those of 18 RUs also at k STAs. Throughputs of 18 RUs also individually double those on 9 RUs at any k STAs.

In addition, when there is no idle RU sensing and the number of STAs is small, the throughputs of the POCW are not better than those of the H-UORA. However, as the number of STAs is larger, its throughputs may be better than the H-UORA's. The POCW outperforms the POCW without RS since sensing idle

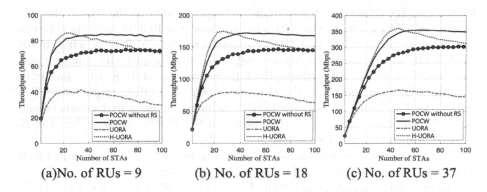

Fig. 5. The system throughputs of the 4 test schemes on overlapping segments given different numbers of RUs, including 9, 18, and 37, and the number of STAs varies from 1 to 100.

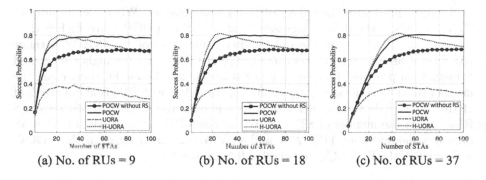

Fig. 6. The success probabilities of the 4 test schemes on overlapping segments given different numbers of RUs, including 9, 18, and 37, and the number of STAs varies from 1 to 100.

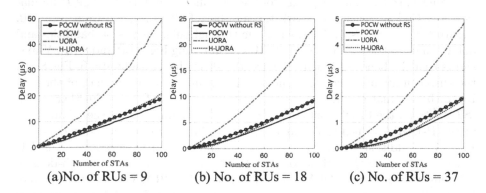

Fig. 7. The delays of the 4 test schemes on overlapping segments given different numbers of RUs, including 9, 18, and 37, and the number of STAs varies from 1 to 100.

RUs during RS time slot actually reduces the probability of idle RUs. When the number of STAs is 100, in the 9-RU environment, the POCW exhibits throughput increases of 16%, 19% and 180% compared to those of POCW without RS, the H-UORA, and the UORA, respectively. Similarly, in an 18-RU environment, the POCW demonstrates a throughput improvements of 16%, 16% and 165% over the POCW without RS, the H-UORA, and the UORA, respectively. Further, in a 37-RU environment, the POCW achieves a throughput enhancements of 16%, 11%, and 139% higher than those of the POCW without RS, the H-UORA, and the UORA, respectively.

The successful transmission rates of the 4 tests schemes are shown in Fig. 6. The UORA reaches only 37% of maximum throughputs as we mentioned before due to transmission collisions. When the number of STA increases, the POCW outperforms the H-UORA. The reason is described above. Actually, higher successful transmission rates will lead to higher throughputs. That is why the treads of Fig. 5.(a), 5.(b), and 5.(c) are similar to those of Fig. 6.(a), 6.(b), and 6.(c), respectively.

Figure 7 illustrates the delays of the 4 test schemes. When the number of STAs is higher, the delays' increasing rates of the H-UORA are higher than those of the POCW, and the delays' increasing rates of the POCW without RU sensing are not higher than those of the H-UORA because higher successful transmission probabilities lead to lower transmission delays. Further, when the number of STAs is the same, e.g., at STAs, the delay of 18 RUs is about one half of that of 37 RUs and the delay of 9 RUs is only about one half of that of 18 RUs. When the number of STAs is 100, in the 9-RU environment, the POCW improves delays about 11%, 20% and 67% compared to those of the POCW without RS, the H-UORA, and the UORA, respectively.

5.3 Experiment on Different Bandwidth of an RU

The third experiment was performed given different bandwidths to an RU, including 6.67 (Modulation and Coding Scheme 5) and 14.7 Mbps (Modulation and Coding Scheme 11) with the number of STAs ranging from 1 to 100. Figure 8, 9 and 10, respectively, show the throughputs, success probabilities and delays on packet size 2K bytes and 9 RUs. Comparing Fig. 8.(a) and 8.(b), Y-axis shows that the bandwidth of an RU greatly affect the throughputs. In Fig. 8.(a), the throughputs of the four schemes are individually about one half of those in Fig. 8.(b), no matter whether at any specific number of STAs. Further, when $|STAs| > 40$, the throughputs of the POCW are significantly higher than those of the H-UORA, which is similar to the cases in the previous experiments (see Fig. 5.). In addition, when $|STAs| > 90$, the throughputs of POCW without RU sensing are higher than those of the H-UORA, implying that in high-density user environments, the POCW outperforms the H-UORA. When $|STAs| = 100$, in 6.67Mbps-bandwidth-of-an-RU environment, the POCW exhibits throughput increases of 15%, 18% and 191% over to the POCW without RS, the H-UORA, and the UORA, respectively. Similarly, in 14.7Mbps-bandwidth-of-an-RU environment, the POCW demonstrates a throughput improvement of 16% over the

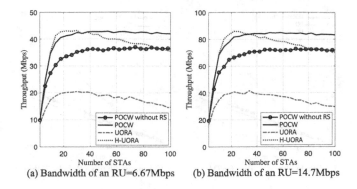

Fig. 8. The system throughputs of the 4 test schemes on overlapping segments given different bandwidths to an RU, including 6.67 and 14.7 Mbps. The number of STAs varies from 1 to 100 and the packet size is 2kB.

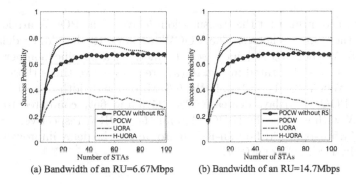

Fig. 9. The success probabilities of the 4 test schemes on overlapping segments given different bandwidth of an RU, including 6.67 and 14.7 Mbps, and the number of STAs varies from 1 to 100.

POCW without RS, 19% increase over the H-UORA, and 180% increase over the UORA. This could be attributed to the POCW's optimization strategies, such as prioritizing data streams based on different access categories and efficient resource allocation, which effectively reduce data transmission collisions and providing higher success probability of data transmission. As $|STAs|$ is larger, the POCW can manage resources and win competition both in a more efficient method, resulting in relatively higher throughputs.

The successful transmission probabilities shown in Fig. 9 reflect the trends of the curves illustrated in Fig. 8. When $|STAs| = 100$, in the 6.67Mbps-bandwidth-of-an-RU environment, the POCW's success probabilities increase 15%, 18% and 196% over the POCW without RS, the H-UORA, and the UORA, respectively. Similarly, in the 14.7Mbps-bandwidth-of-an-RU environment, the improvements are, respectively, 15%, 18% and 185%.

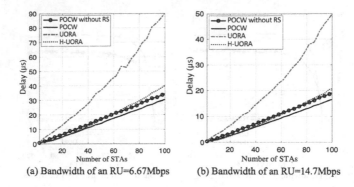

(a) Bandwidth of an RU=6.67Mbps   (b) Bandwidth of an RU=14.7Mbps

Fig. 10. The delays of the 4 test schemes on overlapping segments given different bandwidth of an RU, including 6.67 and 14.7 Mbps, and the number of STAs varies from 1 to 100.

Figure 10 confirms that the transmission delays of the POCW are lower than those of other three schemes. The POCW without RS has lower delays than the H-UORA when $|STAs|$ increases. In fact, at a specific number of STA, e.g., STAs, delays illustrated in Fig. 10.(a) are almost two times those shown in Fig. 10.(b). When $|STAs| = 100$, in the 6.67Mbps-bandwidth-of-an-RU environment, the POCW's delays decrease 12%, 24% and 66% compared to those of the POCW without RS, the H-UORA, and the UORA, respectively. Similarly, in the 14.7Mbps-bandwidth-of-an-RU environment, the delay improvements are, respectively, 11%, 20% and 67%.

6   Conclusions and Future Studies

In this study, we proposed an improved version of the POCW by calculated the appropriate optimal OCW size, adopting RS for RU sensing to reduce the number of idle RUs, and classified data streams, giving them different OCW ranges for priority contention.

Our simulation results showed that comparing with AC_BE and AC_BK, the POCW can provide higher throughputs and lower transmission delays for AC_VO and AC_VI. Our simulations also show that the POCW demonstrates better overall transmission performance, particularly when STAs are densely deployed.

Low-latency networks are crucial for real-time voice/video applications, such as video conferencing and virtual reality, where minimal delays and high reliabilities are essential. Recognizing these demands, IEEE 802.11be is specifically designed to meet the requirements. By offering a network with lower transmission delays, higher transmission rates, and better Quality of Service (QoS), IEEE 802.11be aims to enhance the overall user experience for delay-sensitive applications. To meet the requirements of different data streams and the delay-sensitive nature of IEEE 802.11be, future research will focus on selecting appropriate

OCW ranges in a more flexible and adaptive manner. It is hoped that such studies can provide optimal performance and transmission efficiency in different wireless networks under various network environments and conditions. We will also derive the reliability model and behavior model for the POCW so that user can realize their behaviors and reliabilities before using it. These constitute our future studies.

References

1. Wu, C., Zeng, Y., Zhang, Y.J., Letaief, K.B.: Resource management for ultra-reliable and low-latency communications: an overview. IEEE Wirel. Commun. **26**(1), 108–115 (2019). https://doi.org/10.1109/MWC.2018.1800334
2. Zhu, M., Dai, W., Qiu, M.: A survey of virtual conference systems. IEEE Access **8**, 148756–148769
3. Liu, Y., Guo, Y., Liang, C.: A survey on peer-to-peer video streaming systems. J. Peer-to-Peer Netw. Appl. **1**(1), 18–28 (2008)
4. Al-Fraihat, D., Joy, M., Sinclair, J.: Evaluating E-learning systems success: an empirical study. Comput. Hum. Behav. **102**, 67–86 (2020)
5. Alaa, M., Zaidan, A.A., Zaidan, B.B., Talal, M., Kiah, M.L.M.: A review of smart home applications based on Internet of Things. J. Netw. Comput. Appl. **97**, 48–65
6. Draft Standard for Information Technology - Telecommunications and Information Exchange Between Systems - Part 11: Wireless LAN Medium Access Control (MAC) and Physical Layer (PHY) Specifications - Amendment 6: Enhancements for High Efficiency WLAN D6.0, Draft IEEE Standard, P802.11 (2019)
7. Ghosh, C.: Random access with trigger frames using OFDMA. https://mentor. ieee.org/802.11/dcn/15/11-15-0875-01-00ax-random-accesswith-trigger-frames-using-ofdma.pptx. Accessed 23 Apr 2023
8. Draft Standard for Information Technology - Telecommunications and Information Exchange Between Systems Local and Metropolitan Area Networks-Specific Requirements Part 11: Wireless LAN Medium Access Control (MAC) and Physical (PHY) Specifications Amendment 8: Enhancements for extremely high throughput (EHT), IEEE P802.11be-2022/D2.1, pp. 1–767 (2022)
9. Chang, C.W., Leu, F.Y.: QoS-oriented uplink OFDMA random access scheme for IEEE 802.11be. In: Barolli, L. (eds.) Innovative Mobile and Internet Services in Ubiquitous Computing. IMIS 2023. LNDECT, vol. 177, pp. 32–44. Springer, Cham (2023). https://doi.org/10.1007/978-3-031-35836-4_32
10. Li, X., Wang, Y., Zhang, C., Wu, J., Zhang, J.: Dynamic TXOP reservation for unscheduled on-demand acknowledged service in IEEE 802.11ax WLANs. In: Proceedings of the IEEE International Conference on Communications (ICC) (2019)
11. Choi, J., Jain, M., Meister, J., Sivakumar, R.: Improving 802.11 performance via contention window adaptation. In: Proceedings of the 13th Annual International Conference on Mobile Computing and Networking (MobiCom '07), Montreal, Quebec, Canada, pp. 69–80, September 2007. https://doi.org/10.1145/1287853. 1287862
12. Wang, Y., Thompon, R.S., Vannithamby, R.: Analysis of IEEE 802.11ax association ID assignment for real-time services. In: 2017 IEEE Wireless Communications and Networking Conference Workshops (WCNCW), San Francisco, CA, USA, pp. 1–6, March 2017. https://doi.org/10.1109/WCNCW.2017.7919027

13. Jiyang, B.: Performance Enhancement of IEEE 802.11AX in Ultra-Dense Wireless Networks, Electronic Thesis and Dissertation Repository, p. 5938 (2018). https://ir.lib.uwo.ca/etd/5938

14. Ghosh, C., Stacey, R., Ryu, K., Kim, J., Park, J., Li, Y.: UL OFDMA-based Random Access Parameter Set (RAPS) element, 12 September 2016. https://slideplayer.com/slide/15123174/

15. Chen, T., Zhang, S., Fang, Y., Zhang, J., Wang, W.: Throughput analysis of OFDMA random access with backoff procedure in IEEE 802.11ax networks. IEEE Access **5**, 3833–3846 (2017). https://doi.org/10.1109/ACCESS.2017.2681006

16. Wang, L., Zhu, P., Lin, C., Liu, Y.: Performance analysis of multi-user block acknowledgment in IEEE 802.11ax networks. In: Proceedings of the 2018 IEEE International Conference on Communications (ICC), Kansas City, MO, USA, pp. 1–6, May 2018. https://doi.org/10.1109/ICC.2018.8422157

17. Pedersen, K.I., Heide, J., Mogensen, P.E., Swindlehurst, A.L.: Wireless tactile internet with URLLC: dream or reality? IEEE Trans. Commun. **66**(1), 303–316 (2018). https://doi.org/10.1109/TCOMM.2017.2759630

18. Kim, J., Lee, H., Bahk, S.: CRUI: collision reduction and utilization improvement in OFDMA-based 802.11ax networks. In: IEEE Global Communications Conference (GLOBECOM), pp. 1–6 (2019). https://doi.org/10.1109/GLOBECOM38437.2019.9013337

19. Lanante, L., Uwai, H.O.T., Nagao, Y., Kurosaki, M., Ghosh, C.: Performance analysis of the 802.11ax UL OFDMA random access protocol in dense networks. In: The IEEE International Conference on Communications (ICC), pp. 1–6 (2017). https://doi.org/10.1109/ICC.2017.7997340

20. Lanante, L., Ghosh, C., Roy, S.: Hybrid OFDMA random access with resource unit sensing for next-gen 802.11ax WLANs. IEEE Trans. Mob. Comput. **20**(12), 3338–3350 (2021). https://doi.org/10.1109/TMC.2020.3000503

21. Kim, Y., Lam, K., Park, E.C.: OFDMA backoff control scheme for improving channel efficiency in the dynamic network environment of IEEE 802.11ax WLANs. Sensors **21**(15), 5111 (2021). https://doi.org/10.3390/s21155111

22. Jiang, Z., Li, B., Yang, M., Yan, Z.: Latency oriented OFDMA random access scheme for the next generation WLAN: IEEE 802.11be. In: Lin, Y.B., Deng, D.J. (eds.) Smart Grid and Internet of Things. SGIoT 2020. LNICS, Social Informatics and Telecommunications Engineering, vol. 354, pp. 351–362. Springer, Cham (2021). https://doi.org/10.1007/978-3-030-69514-9_28

A Novel Hierarchical Federated Edge Learning Framework in Satellite-Terrestrial Assisted Networks

Xin-tong Pei[1], Jian-jun Zeng[2], and Zhen-jang Zhang[1]($\boxtimes$)

[1] Key Laboratory of Communication and Information Systems, Beijing Jiaotong, University, Beijing 100044, China
{20111016,zhangzhenjiang}@bjtu.edu.cn
[2] Beijing InchTek Technology, Beijing 100044, China
jj@inchtek.ai

Abstract. On-board federated learning based on dense Low Earth Orbit satellite constellations can meet the data privacy requirements of users in the coverage of non-terrestrial networks. However, traditional satellite-terrestrial assisted federated learning may encounter challenges due to limited satellite resources. To solve the problem, a satellite-terrestrial assisted hierarchical federated edge learning (STA-HFEL) framework is established in this paper. By leveraging well-endowed cloud servers for processing, inter-satellite links, predictability in satellite positioning, and partial aggregation, substantial reductions in training duration and communication costs are achieved. Furthermore, we define a problem within the STA-HFEL framework that involves optimizing the allocation of computation and communication resources for device users to attain overall cost minimization. To address this challenge, we introduce a resource allocation algorithm that operates effectively. Extensive performance evaluations demonstrate that the potential of STA-HFEL as a cost-efficient and privacy-preserving approach for machine learning tasks across distributed remote environments.

Keywords: hierarchical federated learning · LEO satellite network · edge computing · inter-satellite links

1 Introduction

In recent years, the integration of Internet of Things (IoT) technology in remote and underserved regions has shown immense potential for transforming various sectors, from agriculture to healthcare. However, deploying and maintaining traditional IoT infrastructures in these remote areas presents substantial challenges due to connectivity limitations and resource constraints. As a solution to these challenges, LEO satellite communication networks, as a viable complementary alternative to terrestrial networks has emerged. Usually situated between 500 to 2000 km above the Earth's surface, LEO satellite constellation presents advantages such as quicker communication due to reduced

D.-J. Deng and J.-C. Chen (Eds.): SGIoT 2023, LNICST 557, pp. 83–89, 2024.
https://doi.org/10.1007/978-3-031-55976-1_8

propagation latency, decreased energy consumption, and improved signal transmission by enabling more precisely targeted beams to be directed towards the Earth's surface [1]. For out-of-coverage communication targets, inter-satellite links (ISL) enable cross-domain communication [2]. There are numerous challenges waiting to be overcome due to the LEO constellation network's characteristics.

One of the challenges is the strong demand of device data privacy and security. Coined by Google in 2016, a decentralized ML named Federated Learning (FL) allows edge devices to collaboratively train models while keeping their data localized, thus mitigating privacy concerns and reducing communication overhead [3]. By capitalizing on the extensive coverage of satellite networks and their ability to establish connectivity even in regions lacking terrestrial infrastructure, in recent years, there are some explorations on satellite-based FL computing networks. Nasrin Razmi et al. [4] proposed a communication concept specifically adapted to perform a synchronous FL process within a satellite-dense net coordinated by an out-of-constellation PS. It exploits predictability of satellite motion and sub-aggregation to decrease training latency and communication expense. By the same author, [5] modified Federated Averaging algorithm (FedAvg) by leveraging predictive availability of satellites. While effectively reducing training time, this paper converting FedAvg from synchronous to asynchronous learning without compromising training performance. However, excessive model transmission rounds lead to compromised learning performance within the training time limit [6]. This also incurs substantial energy overhead for numerous computation and communication iterations, presenting a challenge for remote-area-devices with low battery capacity, which were not considered in the above studies.

To mitigate such issues, deploying Mobile Edge Computing (MEC) server [7] on the LEO satellite enables the LEO satellite to have the capabilities of aggregated computation and content distribution. Inspired by the hierarchical federated edge learning framework which was proposed by Luo in [8], we proposes STA-HFEL, a dense satellite-terrestrial assisted three-tiers FL edge network, utilizing mediate edge servers on LEO satellites between devices and the remote cloud. Briefly, the main contributions of our work can be summarised as follows:

1) This paper identify the essential hurdles in implementing federated learning on satellites-terrestrial networks for machine learning model training, along with the balance between global transmission overhead and the limited computational processing capacity.

2) We propose a satellite-terrestrial assisted hierarchical federated edge learning (STA-HFEL) framework, offering significant advantages in minimal delay and energy-saving FL for huge scale machine learning tasks in remote areas.

3) With a wide range of numerical experimentation, we showcase that the proposed resource allocation algorithm within the STA-HFEL framework not only outperforms comparative benchmarks in terms of global cost reduction but also exhibits improved training performance compared to the conventional device-cloud-based satellite federated learning approach.

2 Methods

In the STA-HFEL framework, we assume the user devices set as

$$\mathcal{N} = \{n : n = 1, \ldots, N\},\tag{1}$$

the satellite-edge-servers set as

$$\mathcal{K} = \{k : k = 1, \ldots, K\},\tag{2}$$

and a cloud server S. The collection of accessible user devices in communication with edge server i are denoted by $\mathcal{N}_i \in \mathcal{N}$, which is in connection with communication coverage area of satellite i. When user devices are located at considerable distances from each other, they will engage in communication with distinct satellites. Suppose that devices within the communication coverage of the same satellite are located in a compact predefined area, and they share the same geometric configurations with the servicing satellite. For the satellite-to-ground communications, the user device and satellite are visible if

$$\frac{\pi}{2} - \angle(r_{\mathcal{N}_k}, r_k - r_{\mathcal{N}_k}) \geq \alpha_e,\tag{3}$$

where the two vectors in the formula denote the position of device and satellite respectively [9]. The visibility of satellites to a remote cloud fixed on the ground station is also analogous.

In our conceptualization of the STA-HFEL framework, illustrated in Fig. 1, a single training model undergoes the process of model aggregation, occurring both at the satellite edge layer and the cloud layer. Imagine a scenario where user devices stay static while learning, each equipped with a localized data set denoted as $\mathcal{R}_n$. The learning process begins with devices training local models, which are subsequently transmitted to their respective satellite edge servers for aggregation. Upon achieving edge training accuracy, each edge server facilitates global aggregation by transmitting model parameters to the superior layer cloud. This procedure can be outlined as follows.

A. Local model computation

In this step, the objective empirical loss function for device n is defined by the training task as

$$F_n(\theta) = \frac{1}{|\mathcal{R}_n|} \sum_{x \in \mathcal{R}_n} f_n(x; \theta),\tag{4}$$

where $f_n(x; \theta)$ is the training loss for a (labeled) data sample x and model parameters θ. In order to attain a consistent local accuracy $\tau \in (0, 1)$ across all devices for a given model, device n is required to perform a series of local iterations denoted by

$$L(\tau) = \lambda log(1/\tau),\tag{5}$$

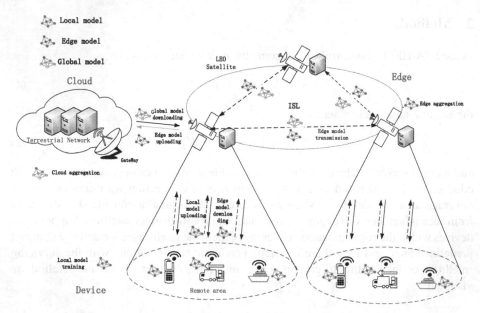

Fig. 1. Satellite-terrestrial assisted hierarchical federated edge learning network

in which λ varies according to data size and computational task [10]. At j-th local iteration, each device, denoted as n, aims to ascertain its local update through the fulfillment of its objective

$$\theta_n^{j+1} = \theta_n^{j+1} - \eta \nabla F(\theta_n^j), \tag{6}$$

Until

$$||\nabla F(\theta_n^{j+1})|| \leq \tau ||\nabla F(\theta_n^j)||, \tag{7}$$

where η represents the predefined learning rate [11].

B. Local model transmission

Upon completing $L(\tau)$ local iterations, local model parameters θ_n^j are send to the designated satellite edge server i, chosen as closest to the device within its visible range. This process also incurs wireless transmission delay and energy.

C. Edge model aggregation

In this stage, every satellite edge server average local parameters as

$$\theta_i = \frac{\sum_{n \in \mathcal{N}_i} |\mathcal{R}_n| \theta_n^j}{|\mathcal{R}_{\mathcal{N}_i}|}, \tag{8}$$

where

$$\mathcal{R}_{\mathcal{N}_i} = \bigcup_{n \in \mathcal{N}_i} \mathcal{R}_n \tag{9}$$

is aggregated data set, and N_i is its attached devices set. Subsequently, each edge server broadcasts θ_i to the devices within N_i for the upcoming iteration in step A. This sequence of steps, spanning from step A to step C, will be iterative repeatedly within satellite edge server i until the attainment of an identical edge accuracy φ, consistent across all satellite edge servers. To attain the specified accuracy of the edge model, the count of iterations at the edge can be deduced as follows [11]:

$$I(\varphi, \tau) = \frac{\sigma \log \frac{1}{\varphi}}{1 - \tau}, \tag{10}$$

where σ is a constant varies with task.

D. Edge model uploading

During this step, edge model parameters are sent from satellites to the remote cloud, typically located on a Ground Station (GS). Only a portion of satellites are linked to the GS, with longer intervals than online time. We address this by using inter-satellite links for model upload. Within orbital levels, satellites form a circular network via ISLs, optimizing connections with adjacent satellites. Communication between GS and satellites is facilitated through the best-connected satellite, guided by orbital mechanics' predictability.

E. Cloud model aggregation

In the ultimate stage of this process, the cloud acquires model parameters from each satellite edge and proceeds to aggregation these models as

$$\theta = \frac{\sum_{i \in \mathcal{K}} |\mathcal{R}_{N_i}| \theta_i}{|\mathcal{R}|}, \tag{11}$$

where

$$\mathcal{R} = \bigcup_{i \in \mathcal{K}} \mathcal{R}_{N_i} \tag{12}$$

is aggregated data set under cloud S. To offer a clearer depiction, Algorithm 1 presents a step-by-step procedure for one global iteration.

Algorithm 1: STA-HFEL iterative process

Input: Device initial model set $\left\{\theta^0_{n \in \mathcal{N}}\right\}$, with local iteration j = 0, local
accuracy τ, edge accuracy φ
Output: global model θ
for j *in range(I$(\varphi, \tau)L(\tau)$)* **do**
    for *device n in range(N)* **do**
        ⌊ Solve problem (6) and derive θ^j_n (Step A);
    Devices send refreshed θ^j_n to satellite edge server (Step B);
    if $j\%L(\tau) = 0$ **then**
        for *satellite edge i in range (K)* **do**
            i received $\{\theta^j_n : n \in \mathcal{N}_i\}$ and calculate θ_i with Eq. (8), deriving θ_i
            (Step C);
            i broadcast θ_i to devices in $\mathcal{N}_i$ such that $\theta^j_n = \theta_i$ for each $n \in \mathcal{N}_i$;

  i transmit $\{\theta_{i \in \mathcal{K}}\}$ with intra-plane ISLs to GS (Step D);
Cloud S got $\{\theta_{i \in \mathcal{K}}\}$, to fix (11) and obtains global θ (Step E);

---

3 Results

We evaluate our proposed algorithms from Section II using logistic regression on the MNIST dataset [12] and compare it to the conventional device-cloud-based FedAvg model. Our study employs a walker constellation with 40 LEO satellites across 5 orbital planes at an 80° inclination, with a GS situated at the North Pole. We involve 30 devices under each satellite in the training process, with datasets partitioned into 75% for training and 25% for testing.

Results indicate our STA-HFEL algorithm surpasses FedAvg by around 5% in both test and training accuracy, with a 3% reduction in training loss. This is attributed to STA-HFEL's multiple edge-based model aggregation rounds alongside local iterations within a global iteration, offering enhanced learning benefits. In contrast, FedAvg relies solely on local datasets during global iterations without external network integration.

The cost-saving effectiveness of STA-HFEL is also assessed. With $\tau = 0.9$ local accuracy and $\varphi = 0$ edge accuracy, STA-HFEL is compared against traditional device-cloud-based satellite FL models. It demonstrates notable improvements in iteration count, reducing iterative model parameter transmission costs compared to the classic approach.

4 Conclusions

We propose a comprehensive framework for a three-tiers hierarchical federated edge learning model that leverages satellite-terrestrial assisted communication to facilitate efficient knowledge exchange and model improvement to enable great potentials in cost-efficient application of FL in remote-area-IoT. Through partially migrating model aggregation from the cloud to edge servers, our suggested STA-HFEL method converges to a steady system state, surpassing the designated benchmarks in global energy reduction and exhibiting superior training performance over traditional on-board FL approaches for satellites.

Ultimately, as demonstrated by our simulation results, the STA-HFEL framework achieves higher global and test accuracy, along with lower training loss, in comparison to traditional satellite federated learning devoid of intermediate layer aggregation.

References

1. Chen, H., Xiao, M., Pang, Z.B.: Satellite-based computing networks with federated learning. IEEE Wirel. Commun. **29**(1), 78–84 (2022)
2. Wang, F., Jiang, D., Qi, S., Qiao, C., Shi, L.: A dynamic resource scheduling scheme in edge computing satellite networks. Mobile Networks and Applications **26**, 597–608 (2021)
3. Konecny, J., et al.: Federated learning: Strategies for improving communication efficiency. NIPS Workshop on Private Multi-Party Machine Learning (2016)
4. Razmi, N., Matthiesen, B., Dekorsy, A., Popovski, P.: On-Board Federated Learning for Dense LEO Constellations. In: ICC 2022 - IEEE International Conference on Communications, pp. 4715–4720. IEEE, Seoul, Korea (2022)
5. Razmi, N., Matthiesen, B., Dekorsy, A., Popovski, P.: Ground-assisted federated learning in LEO satellite constellations. IEEE Wireless Communications Letters **11**(4), 717–721 (2022)
6. Sviridenko, M.: A note on maximizing a submodular set function subject to a knapsack constraint. Oper. Res. Lett. **32**(1), 41–43 (2004)
7. Shi, W.S., Cao, J., Zhang, Q., Li, Y.H.S., Xu, L.Y.: Edge Computing: Vision and Challenges. IEEE Internet of Things Journal **3**(5), 637–646 (2016)
8. Luo, S.Q., Chen, X., Wu, Q., Zhou, Z., Yu, S.: HFEL: Joint Edge Association and Resource Allocation for Cost-Efficient Hierarchical Federated Edge Learning. IEEE Trans. Wireless Commun. **19**(10), 6535–6548 (2020)
9. So, J., et al.: FedSpace: an efficient federated learning framework at satellites and ground stations. Computer Science (2022)
10. Dinh, C.T., et al.: Federated learning over wireless networks: convergence analysis and resource allocation. IEEE/ACM Transactions on Networking **29**(1), 398–409 (2021)
11. Ma, C.X., et al.: Distributed optimization with arbitrary local solvers. Optimization Methods and Software **32**(4), 813–848 (2017)
12. Li, T., Sahu, A.K., Zaheer, M., Sanjabi, M., Talwalkar, A., Smith, V.: Federated optimization in heterogeneous networks. Proceedings of Machine learning and systems **2**, 429–450 (2020)

Cell Clusters and Their Networks
for Emerging Applications

Tadashi Nakano[1]($\boxtimes$) (iD) and Tatsuya Suda[2]

[1] Osaka Metropolitan University, Osaka, Japan
tnakano@omu.ac.jp
[2] University Net Group Inc., P.O.Box 1288, Fallbrook, CA 92088, USA

Abstract. Cell clusters and networks that interconnect them are key components of emerging applications such as 6G wireless molecular communication systems, drug delivery and tissue regeneration. This paper discusses empirical, analytical and simulation-based approaches towards understanding how spatially distributed cells aggregate to form cell clusters and how formed cell clusters grow and form a network that interconnects themselves. In order to illustrate these different approaches, this paper also describes authors' previous work relating to these approaches.

Keywords: Cell cluster · cell cluster network · cell spheroid · emerging application

1 Introduction

In emerging interdisciplinary applications such as 6G wireless molecular communication systems [1], drug delivery [2], tissue regeneration [3], bio-robotics [4], and organs-on-chips [5], biological cells and the clusters they form, as well as networks that interconnect cell clusters, are key components of the applications. A cell cluster is a three-dimensional aggregate of biological cells that is formed via cell-cell adhesion of individual cells. In applications, cell clusters communicate and coordinate with each other through exchanging molecules and perform application related functionalities.

In biology, spatially distributed cells exchange bio-chemical molecules, coordinate their movement, aggregate and form cell clusters. For instance, Dictyostelium discoideum cells exchange cAMP (cyclic adenosine monophosphate) molecules, move toward each other, and form clusters that rotate [6]. Endothelial cells exchange VEGF (vascular endothelial growth factor) molecules, move toward each other, and form cell clusters and a network that interconnects the clusters [7]. Cancer cells divide, increase in their numbers, and form cell clusters that perform collective invasion [8].

This work was supported by JSPS KAKENHI Grant Numbers JP18KK0314 and JP22K19780.

In biomedical engineering, various techniques have been developed for the creation of cell clusters known as cell spheroids. The commonly employed technique utilizes a culture plate with a non-adhesive surface to prevent cells from adhering to the plate and to facilitate cell aggregation. Efforts are currently underway to develop techniques for establishing a network of cell spheroids. In [9], for instance, motor neuron spheroids are inter-connected through co-culturing with endothelial cells.

When cell clusters communicate and process information in a cooperative manner, it could help implement emerging interdisciplinary applications. For instance, drug delivery applications may benefit from having two types of the cell cluster in the environment and having them communicate. "Sensing" clusters detect specific bio-marker molecules in the environment, and "therapeutic" clusters produce therapeutic molecules. Upon detecting the presence of bio-marker molecules, sensing clusters send information to therapeutic clusters, which in turn produce therapeutic molecules.

The goal of this paper is to discuss empirical, analytic and simulation-based approaches to understanding how cells may form cell clusters and how cell clusters may form a network. In Sect. 2, we discuss empirical approaches and describe our preliminary wet laboratory experiments and demonstrate the feasibility of developing networks that interconnect spatially distributed cell clusters. We then discuss analytical approaches in Sect. 3 and simulation-based approaches in Sect. 4. Finally, in Sect. 5, we discuss future research challenges.

2   Wet Laboratory Experiments

An empirical (or experimental) approach enables observing, in the natural setting, how cells form a cluster and how such cell clusters form a network and communicate.

At the same time, the empirical approach presents its own challenges. For instance, although one can observe through biological experiments biological phenomena as they take place in a natural environment, it alone may not be sufficient to understand underlying mechanisms that cause what is being observed. Experimental protocols need to be established such that other researchers can reproduce experimental results. Types of cells available for biological experiments, i.e., types of cells whose basic behaviors have been experimentally established, may be limited. Many existing biological experiments are conducted in a 2D environment, and conducting biological experiments and observing experimental results in a more realistic 3D environment are not straightforward. Many studies report that cells behave differently in the 2D environment and 3D environment.

In the following, we briefly describe our empirical approach to understanding how cells form a cluster and how such cell clusters form a network.

To form a network of cell clusters, we first prepare cell clusters using EZSPHERE (AGC Techno Glass Inc., Shizuoka, Japan). We then transfer cell clusters to 35-mm glass-bottom dishes (Matsunami Glass, Kishiwada, Japan)

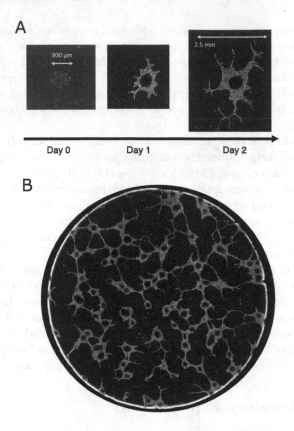

Fig. 1. Experimental results [10]. (A) A growing cell cluster at days 0, 1 and 2. (B) A cell cluster network interconnecting multiple cell clusters observed at day 3. The diameter of the circular area, 14 mm.

in Dulbecco's Modified Eagle Medium supplemented with 10% fetal calf serum where a layer of Matrigel (8–12 mg/mL; Falcon), a gelatinous protein mixture resembling the extracellular environment in tissue, is formed. We incubate the dishes at 37 °C under 5% CO_2 for 3–5 days, while we obtain phase contrast images every 24 h.

Figure 1 shows experimental results obtained in our previous work [10]. Figure 1(A) shows how a cell cluster grew. In this biological experiment, we first placed a (3D) spherical cell cluster of approximately 300 μm in diameter on Matrigel and observed how this cell cluster grew. As shown in the figure, the cell cluster grew as the cells inside the cluster moved, changed their morphology and divided. It grew to a size of about 2.5 mm while forming multiple needle-like arm structures over a period of 2 days.

Figure 1(B) shows a cell cluster network interconnecting multiple cell clusters. In this experiment, multiple cell clusters were first placed on Matrigel. We then observed that cell clusters constantly changed their shapes and extended multiple needle-like arm structures; when these needle-like arm structures from different cell clusters encounter in the environment, they physically attach to each other and form a network that interconnects spatially distributed cell clusters.

3 Analytical Approaches

Analytical approaches allow one to focus on key system factors and ignore non critical factors, form and test a hypothesis regarding how cells form a cluster and how formed clusters communicate, and adjust the hypothesis based on the analytical results. Biological experiments should guide the choice of critical system factors to consider in the analytic approaches and hypothesis to form and test.

Analytical approaches may be either microscopic or macroscopic, depending on the level of abstraction. Microscopic models describe the state of each individual system entity. Macroscopic models describe the global state of the system. Microscopic and macroscopic models complement each other, as they describe dynamics at different levels.

3.1 Microscopic Modelling

Microscopic models describe the state of each individual system entity. For instance, using the Langevin equation [11], which was originally developed to describe the Brownian motion of a particle, movement of a system entity i (say, cell i) in a one dimensional space may be described in the following manner.

$$m\frac{\mathrm{d}v_i}{\mathrm{d}t} = -\lambda v_i + \xi(t), \tag{1}$$

where cells move in a one-dimensional space, and the moving velocity v_i of cell $i \in \mathcal{N}$ is the variable of the equation and changes according to the above stochastic differential equation. On the left-hand side of (1), m is the mass of the cell, while on the right-hand side of (1), λ is a positive constant, and λv represents the resistance to the cell's motion. $\xi(t)$ represents a noise and follows a Gaussian probability distribution with zero mean $\langle \xi(t) \rangle = 0$ and correlation $\langle \xi(t_1) \cdot \xi(t_2) \rangle = 2\lambda k_B T \delta(t_1 - t_2)$, where k_B is Boltzmann's constant, T is the absolute temperature, and $\delta(\cdot)$ is the Dirac delta function.

3.2 Macroscopic Modelling

In contrast to the microscopic models described above, macroscopic models describe the global state of the system such as the number or concentration of cells. Macroscopic models usually take the form of a set of partial differential equations (PDEs).

Assume that cells move in a one-dimensional space, and let $c(x,t)$ be the concentration of cells at position x at time t. Using a diffusion equation, the rate of change in $c(x,t)$ is given by

$$\frac{\partial c(x,t)}{\partial t} = D\frac{\partial^2 c(x,t)}{\partial x^2} - \frac{\partial}{\partial x}\left[c(x,t)G(x)\right],\tag{2}$$

where D is the diffusion coefficient of cells, and G is a drift term. G can be used to describe the directed motion of cells. In the case of chemotactic bacteria, G becomes a function of attractant concentration and gradient of the attractant concentration [12] and is given as $G(x) \propto \chi(c_a)\frac{\partial c_a}{\partial x}$, where c_a is the attractant concentration at position x, and $\chi(c_a)$ is in the form of a Michaelis-Menten equation [13].

4   Simulation-Based Approaches

When a model increases its complexity, analytical solutions are often unavailable. In such cases, simulations-based approaches provide tractable alternatives.

A simulation is an imitation of the real-world process. Simulations require a model that represents the key behavior of the selected system element(s), and the simulation numerically calculates the evolution of the model over time. To conduct simulations, the time in the model equations is discretized, and the continuous-time model equations such as (1) and (2) become discrete-time difference equations, when necessary. Given initial conditions, then, the model equations are solved numerically to obtain the state of the selected system element(s) (e.g., the position of each and every cell or spatial cell distribution) at time t incrementally from time $t = 0$.

Simulation models can be classified into *off-lattice* and *on-lattice* models [14]: on-lattice models track cells along a rigid grid and off-lattice models have no such restriction. An agent-based model (ABM) [10] is an example of the former, and the Cellular Potts Model (CPM) is an example of the latter.

An Agent-Based Model. In the agent-based modelin our earlier study [10], each cell is an individual object and moves based on a set of forces it receives. In cells forming a cluster, we consider two types of force that acts on the cells: the attractive force and the repulsive force. Both the attractive force and the repulsive force acts between cells. The attractive force acts in a long-range, allowing cells at distance to move toward each other. The repulsive force acts in a short-range, allowing cells in their close proximity to move away from each other. The two types of force determine the size of the cluster that cells form.

In the wet-laboratory experiments in our earlier study shown in Fig. 1(A), some cells at the periphery of a cluster moved away from the cluster and other nearby cells followed the cells moving away from the cluster; as a result, the cluster grew multiple branches. In collective cell migration [15,16], such cells moving away from the cluster they belong to are called *leaders*, while others are

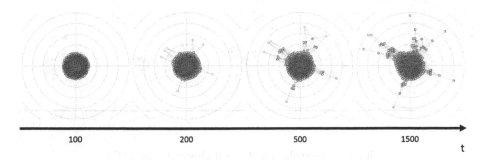

100   200   500   1500

t

Fig. 2. Time evolution of a cell cluster in the agent-based simulation [10]

called *followers*. Leaders have free edges or more extensive substrate interactions than followers. In our model [10], cell i acts as a leader when it is in physical contact with a small number of cells at time t; otherwise, cell i acts as a follower. Leaders and followers use different types of force to move: the forward force and following force, respectively.

Figure 2 shows a simulation result obtained using our agent model. At time $t = 0$, 500 cells formed a cluster. At time $t = 100$, cells differentiated into leaders (colored) and followers (gray). Leaders then move away from the cluster center while followers follow them so that a cluster grows and extends its branches (at time $t = 200$, 500 and 1500).

Cellular Pots Model (CPM). In another simulation-based study of ours, we employed the Cellular Pots Model (CPM). The CPM is a discrete-time simulation model that represents cells or cell population on a regular and orthogonal grid [17]. In CPM, each cell is assigned a numerical ID, and it is represented as a set of lattice sites with the same numerical ID, unlike agent-based models, which treat each cell as an individual object. CPM is suitable to reproduce complex cell shapes such as those in Fig. 1.

In CPM [17], a cell is represented by a collection of lattice sites. A cell with label N ($1 \leq N \leq M$) is represented by a collection of all lattice sites to which a numerical ID of N is assigned (i.e., all lattice sites i for which $\sigma_i = N$). Here, M is the total number of cells.

In CPM, there is an energy E associated with a given arrangement of cells.

$$E = \sum_{i,j} J_{\sigma_i \sigma_j}(1 - \delta_{\sigma_i \sigma_j})$$
$$+ \sum_{N=1}^{M} \kappa(A_N - A_0)^2 + \sum_{N=1}^{M} \gamma(L_N - L_0)^2 \qquad (3)$$

Noting that $\delta_{\sigma_i \sigma_j}$ is the Kronecker delta, which takes the value of 1 if $\sigma_i = \sigma_j$ and 0 otherwise. The first term in the above equation represents the energy concerning the cell-cell interaction and is calculated only for the lattice sites

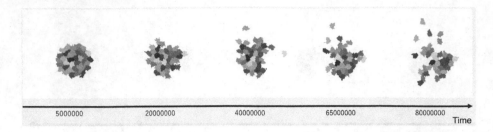

Fig. 3. Time evolution of a cell cluster in the CPM

located at the boundary of a cell to its adjacent cells. The second term and third term in the above equation represent the energy concerning the area elasticity and that concerning the perimeter elasticity of the cell, respectively. κ and γ in these terms are constants and determine the energy. A_N and L_N in these terms represent the area and perimeter of cell N. The substrate in which no cells reside is represented by lattice sites labeled with 0. A_0 and L_0 are the target area and target perimeter. The sum in the second and third terms is calculated for all cells on the lattice.

In simulations, we select a randomly chosen lattice site i. If it is located at the boundary of cell N, we select one of the lattice sites, say lattice site j, adjacent to site i. We calculate the difference ΔE between the energy before making the lattice site j identical to the lattice site i and after doing so, and compute the probability P_r of whether this change should take place using the following equation.

$$P_r = \begin{cases} 1 & (\Delta E \leq 0) \\ \exp\left(-\Delta E/T\right) & (\Delta E > 0) \end{cases} \tag{4}$$

The symbol T is a constant referred to as the temperature of the simulation in CPM and determines the transition probability P_r when $\Delta E > 0$.

Figure 3 shows the simulation result obtained using the CPM in our earlier study. In our earlier study, we extended the CPM in order to reproduce characteristics of cells observed in biological experiments. In our extended CPM model, cells at the periphery of the cluster probabilistically moved away from the cluster. Once cells started moving away from the cluster, they maintained the direction of movement, and other nearby cells followed them to form a narrow and long needle-like arm structures. This resulted in a cluster with a complex-shape as shown in the figure. Our extended CPM model reproduced some features of a cell cluster observed in wet-laboratory experiments in Fig. 1.

5   Future Work

One of the key future challenges is to identify how cell clusters and their networks may be used to implement emerging applications.

Applications that may benefit from cell clusters and the network that interconnects them include regenerative medicine, neural spheroid networks, and brain science. For instance, in the regenerative medicine application, cell clusters may communicate and coordinate their movement with other cell clusters to form a 3D structure of a given internal organ. In the neural spheroid network application, cell clusters (representing a group of neurons) may communicate and coordinate with other cell clusters through narrow needle-like links of cells. Neural spheroid networks may also be linked with networks comprising of other types of cells, such as endothelial cells, to establish an experimental model of the human brain to help study human brain functions.

References

1. Guo, W., et al.: Molecular physical layer for 6G in wave-denied environments. IEEE Commun. Mag. **59**(5), 33–39 (2021)
2. Kitada, T., DiAndreth, B., Teague, B., Weiss, R.: Programming gene and engineered-cell therapies with synthetic biology. Science **359**(6376) (2018)
3. Teague, B.P., Guye, P., Weiss, R.: Synthetic morphogenesis. Cold Spring Harb. Perspect. Biol. **8**(9), a023929 (2016)
4. Kamm, R.D., et al.: Perspective: the promise of multi-cellular engineered living systems. APL Bioeng. **2**(4), 040901 (2018)
5. Low, L.A., Mummery, C., Berridge, B.R., Austin, C.P., Tagle, D.A.: Organs-on-chips: into the next decade. Nat. Rev. Drug Discov. **20**, 345–361 (2021)
6. Weijer, C.J.: Collective cell migration in development. J. Cell Sci. **122**(18), 3215–3223 (2009)
7. Czirok, A.: Endothelial cell motility, coordination and pattern formation during vasculogenesis. Wiley Interdiscip. Rev. Syst. Biol. Med. **5**(5), 587–602 (2013)
8. Friedl, P., Gilmour, D.: Collective cell migration in morphogenesis, regeneration and cancer. Nat. Rev. Mol. Cell Biol. **10**(7), 445–457 (2009)
9. Osaki, T., Sivathanu, V., Kamm, R.D.: Engineered "3D" vascular and neuronal networks in a microfluidic platform. Sci. Rep. **8**(1), 5168 (2018)
10. Matsushita, K., Nakano, T.: Wet-laboratory experiments and computer simulation of growing cell clusters. In: GLOBECOM 2022-2022 IEEE Global Communications Conference, pp. 4541–4546 (2022)
11. Nakano, T., et al.: Performance evaluation of leader-follower-based mobile molecular communication networks for target detection applications. IEEE Trans. Commun. **65**(2), 663–676 (2017)
12. Keller, E.F., Segel, L.A.: Model for chemotaxis. J. Theor. Biol. **30**, 225–234 (1971)
13. Keener, J., Sneyd, J.: Mathematical Physiology II: Systems Physiology. Springer, New York (2008). https://doi.org/10.1007/978-0-387-79388-7
14. Metzcar, J., Wang, Y., Heiland, R., Macklin, P.: A review of cell-based computational modeling in cancer biology. JCO Clin. Cancer Inform. **3** (2019)
15. Rørth, P.: Fellow travellers: emergent properties of collective cell migration. EMBO Rep. **13**(11), 984–991 (2012)
16. Qin, L., Yang, D., Yi, W., Cao, H., Xiao, G.: Roles of leader and follower cells in collective cell migration. Mol. Biol. Cell **32**(14), 1267–1272 (2021)
17. Hirashima, T., Rens, E.G., Merks, R.M.H.: Cellular potts modeling of complex multicellular behaviors in tissue morphogenesis. Dev. Growth Differ. **59**(5), 329–339 (2017)

Protocol, Algorithm, Services
and Applications

Cluster-Based Optimization Method
for Delivery Networks

Cheng-Hui Chen[1]([⊠]), Yen-Shiuan Lin[2], Yung-Kuan Chan[2], and Shyr-Shen Yu[1]

[1] Department of Computer Science and Engineering, National Chung Hsing University,
Taichung City 407224, Taiwan
star90154@gmail.com
[2] Department of Management Information Systems, National Chung Hsing University,
Taichung City 407224, Taiwan

Abstract. Traditional logistics scheduling, which heavily relies on experienced personnel, can be time-consuming and prone to oversights, issues that are further amplified with the integration of new distributors. Addressing these challenges, this study proposes a unique cluster-based optimization method for delivery networks (COMDN). COMDN leverages extensive RFID signal data, incorporating delivery locations, spatial zones, and delivery priorities, among others. The process begins by collecting delivery locations and computing pairwise distances between distributors, followed by the clustering of suppliers based on these distances. The final stage involves constructing an optimal delivery route, assisting in distribution to diverse, dispersed, and complex locations on the map, thereby ensuring a balanced delivery to each location and establishing shorter delivery paths. This results in a significant reduction in order processing times. Using data from a prominent tobacco and alcohol distributor in central Taiwan, the study implements shipment scheduling and route optimization. Experimental results reveal that COMDN, when compared to previous manual methods, shows a significant 2.98% improvement over existing procedures, demonstrating its efficiency and applicability in a wide range of multi-objective delivery and logistics scenarios.

Keywords: Route Optimization · Delivery Networks · Vehicle Allocation

1 Introduction

Traditional logistics, focused primarily on the spatiotemporal displacement of goods, aids in bridging the gap between the production and consumption sites of products. This logistics modality encompasses storage, transportation, and auxiliary services associated with goods handling [1]. From a managerial perspective, cultivating proficient employees in warehousing and transportation demands extensive training, often spanning years. However, frequent personnel transitions impede the effective transfer and accumulation of experience, necessitating constant training for new recruits. Furthermore, internal coordination within enterprises presents considerable challenges, occasionally resulting in communicational discrepancies or conflicts.

© ICST Institute for Computer Sciences, Social Informatics and Telecommunications Engineering 2024
Published by Springer Nature Switzerland AG 2024. All Rights Reserved
D.-J. Deng and J.-C. Chen (Eds.): SGIoT 2023, LNICST 557, pp. 101–112, 2024.
https://doi.org/10.1007/978-3-031-55976-1_10

The transformation from traditional to modern logistics has been accelerated by economic growth and technological advancements. Modern logistics, which are underpinned by state-of-the-art information technology, consolidate transportation, handling, shipping, warehousing, distribution, recovery, and logistics information processing. As a departure from traditional logistics, which is anchored in manufacturing processes, modern logistics foregrounds customer service, underscoring the customer-centric orientation of logistics operations. Two core tenets underlie modern logistics: emphasis on customer service and prioritization of transportation and storage operations. In this context, enterprises are now tasked with addressing the critical challenge of swiftly responding to customer needs and abbreviating order processing lead times [2].

This study presents a cluster-based optimization method for delivery networks (COMDN). This methodology unfolds over three stages. The first stage involves the collection of delivery locations and the computation of pairwise distances between distributors. The subsequent stage focuses on clustering different suppliers based on these distances. In the final stage, an optimal delivery route is constructed. This method aids in distributing to numerous, dispersed, and complex locations on the map, enabling balanced delivery to each location and creating shorter delivery paths. This ultimately reduces order processing times. COMDN can be applied in a wide array of multi-objective delivery and logistics scenarios.

In the past few years, there has been a lot of research on time and capacity constrained vehicle scheduling and routing problems. The Vehicle Scheduling Problem saw the adoption of a Hybrid Genetic Algorithm (HGAV) [1]. This algorithm combines the greedy interchange local optimization algorithm, which requires that all nodes be assigned to vehicles for the minimum vehicle scheduling cost of moving goods from warehouse to arrival. The total travel time, the total delay time and the minimization of the number of trucks are considered, and a feasible solution is found after implementation.

Traditional delivery trucks, possessing a substantial load capacity, do not typically return to the warehouse before completing all customer visits [4]. However, factors such as terrain and traffic conditions may limit the number of customers that can be served. As a result, some e-commerce and logistics companies are now implementing a dual-delivery system using both drones and trucks for efficient distribution. The daily distribution of cartons from collection stations, a unique vehicle routing problem, was addressed by [5]. Because cartons are a special product with a short production cycle, they hope to provide a small number of cartons every day, for the carton factory, they need to get the maximum profit while satisfying customer demand. Due to the high delivery costs for customers who order a small number of cartons per day, carton factories assign delivery tasks to third-party logistics companies to reduce their operating costs. This problem can be solved by using Particle Swarm Optimization (PSO) to deliver cartons from multiple carton factories to a collection station, and then arranging vehicles from the collection station to deliver cartons to the customer. This problem can save about 28% of the total delivered cost, and compared with the actual example, it can significantly reduce the number of vehicles required.

In real life, certain types of transportation have strict time limits. When the delivery man sets out, not only the capacity of the vehicle should be considered, but also the demand of time. These two papers both belong to the Vehicle Routing Problem with Time Window (VRPTW), which is more complex than the traditional VRP and one of the most important branches of VRP. Research explored a scenario in which every customer receives a visit once to secure goods within a specified time limit [6]. The goal is to minimize the total cost, an improved artificial bee colony algorithm (IABC) is used to solve the problem. To tackle the issue of food delivery in Dalian, China [7]. In order to maintain the freshness of food, there are strict requirements on the delivery time. IABC is used as the solution to develop an integrated linear model, which is mainly to provide the lowest cost path for all customers within the time, and it needs to meet the constraints of service time and vehicles [8]. The results show that the IABC algorithm can effectively solve the vehicle routing problem with time window.

In the above-mentioned literature on all employee scheduling problems, whether VSP, VRP or VRPTW problems, they are all considered as non-deterministic polynomial time hard (NP-hard) problem [9]. When confronting complex or large-scale problems, the time taken to find a solution can increase exponentially due to constraints or variable length, making it challenging to find the optimal solution within a reasonable timeframe. In practical applications, swift results are often desired over the absolute optimal solution. Thus, the aim is to identify a superior feasible solution within an effective time window. Various methods such as genetic algorithms, artificial bee colony algorithms, or particle swarm optimization can be employed to tackle such problems.

The paper is structured as follows: Sect. 2 delves into the collection and processing of delivery data, and the methodology for optimizing delivery routes. Section 3 examines the application of the experimental method to real-world scenarios. Finally, Sect. 4 rounds off the discussion with the conclusion, highlighting the contributions of this delivery scheduling study and illuminating potential paths for future research.

2 Materials and Methods

This study presents a cluster-based optimization method for delivery networks (COMDN). COMDN unfolds over three stages. The first stage involves the collection of delivery locations and the computation of pairwise distances between distributors. The subsequent stage focuses on clustering different suppliers based on these distances. In the final stage, an optimal delivery route is constructed.

2.1 Problem Description

In this study, the logistics and distribution scheduling of the case company is discussed. In order to reduce the cost of transportation, the appropriate objective function is set according to different problems and needs, and the appropriate scheduling is finally planned, so that the transportation can be smoother and the overall time can be shortened. In traditional transportation and delivery, the delivery arrangement is made manually according to the customer's order and the delivery location, but it will cost too much manpower and time, and the artificial judgment undistributed is inevitable. Therefore, this study proposes a logistics delivery system to assist operational staff in managing dispatch-related tasks. After identifying the dealerships to which deliveries must be made each day, it is necessary to schedule vehicle dispatches. Crucially, decisions must be made regarding which dealerships each van should service each day. To optimize convenience and reduce fuel costs, nearby dealerships are grouped together and assigned to the same van. As such, this necessitates the design of a novel vehicle allocation and delivery routing method.

2.2   Data Acquisition and Content Description

In the proposed method, a wide range of delivery data is collected through RFID signals. The information acquired includes:

1. Dealer Location: The GPS coordinates (longitude and latitude) of each dealer are gathered.
2. Spatial Area Location: GPS positioning is employed to dynamically cluster different dealer areas.
3. Dealer ID: This unique identifier is used for each dealer.
4. Dealer Ranking: The dealers are categorized into four ranks based on their operational scale and sales performance. The ranks are: Level 1, Level 2, Level 3, and Level 4. The frequency of product delivery to these ranks is as follows: 1 delivery for Level 1, 3 deliveries for Level 2, 2 deliveries for Level 3, and 1 delivery for Level 4.

The final computations are transmitted to the individual delivery driver's mobile device via a WiFi network, facilitating the completion of the delivery tasks. This system allows for efficient scheduling and routing, ensuring that deliveries are made according to the priority levels of the dealers.

2.3   Vehicle Allocation

This section outlines the process of determining the distribution of dealerships to each delivery van and establishing the delivery schedules for each van. Typically, in the allocation of dealerships, those that are geographically close are assigned to the same delivery van to facilitate transportation efficiency. Conversely, dealerships that are situated at a greater distance from one another are handled by different vans to maximize the breadth of delivery coverage.

Shortest Distance

In this study, the shortest distance between the two dealers was automatically calculated by Google Map. There are many applications that use Google Maps for navigation or geographic information systems. With the Google Maps Application Programming Interface (API), which can link applications, data, and hardware. An integrated system that feeds back relative information and interacts with the user's purpose, providing many functions, including the Google Place API, which is used to build location-based service applications [10].

Suppose S_a is the dataset of dealers to be visited on the same day, where each element contains the dealer to be visited, represented by $S_a[i].Dealer$. The graph dist is described by an $n_w \times n_w$ matrix, where $dist[i, j]$ represents the shortest distance between the ith dealer and the jth dealer. The following pseudo code is the graphical dist created by using Google map to calculate the distance between each dealer, as shown in Algorithm Distance section.

Algorithm Distance

---

1.   googlemaps.Client(key=api_key) // google map api

2.   dist = [][] // create empty array

3.   for i to range($length_{data}$):

4.   for j to range(i+1, $length_{data}$):

5.   distance = calculation of distance // The shortest distance between the ith and jth dealers

6.   dist[i][j] = distance

Cluster

In this study, after calculating the distance between two dealers, it is then necessary to assign each truck to deliver the products to those dealers. The purpose of clustering is to complete the delivery of all goods without spending too much delivery time and cost. Therefore, the delivery time and cost of delivery can be reduced if dealers with similar distance are delivered by the same truck. In contrast, dealers at the two locations furthest apart are usually assigned to different trucks for shipment during delivery schedules.

The COMDN algorithm is designed to find N_c reference points for N_c trucks and to find. First, two dealers with the farthest distance are found from dist as the benchmark. If N_c is greater than 2, which means there are more than two trucks, then the distance between the dealer and the base dealer must be greater than Th_d, and the sum of the distances between the dealer and the benchmark dealer is the largest, as the new benchmark dealer. The N_c dealers obtained through this algorithm are transported by N_c trucks, which are used as the benchmark for each truck. The pseudocode for COMDN is demonstrated in the Algorithm COMDN section.

Algorithm COMDN
1.   benchmark = [ ] // create an empty array to store the dealer as a benchmark
2.   dist[i,j] = find the two dealers who are furthest away
3. Th_d = dist[i,j] × 0.9
4.   benchmark = {i, j}
5.   the distance between i and j is set to infinity
6.   count = 2
7.   while count < N_c :
8.   k = The distance between the dealer and the benchmark is greater than the Th_d, and the distance from the benchmark is the largest
9.   benchmark = benchmark ∪ {k}
10.   count = count + 1
11. $Th_d = Th_d × 0.9$

Next, the N_a dealers are divided into N_c groups, and each group represents the group of dealers who order products to be delivered by a truck. Therefore, the Partition algorithm designed in this study requires that the number of dealers responsible for delivering products of each truck can be evenly distributed. In addition, consideration is also given to the proximity of the dealer's products, as far as possible can be transported by the same truck. According to the base dealer identified by COMDN's algorithm and assigned to the dealers nearest to the benchmark until all the dealers are arranged. The pseudocode is presented in the Algorithm Partition.

Algorithm Partition
1.   for i = 0 to $length_{benchmark}$:
2.   dealer[i] = benchmark[i]
3.   total[i] = 1
4.   iteration = 0
5.   while (iteration < $length_{N_a}$ - $length_{benchmark}$):
6. $j = \arg(Min_{i=0}^{Nc-1} total[i])$
7.   From N_a, the closest dealer k to dealer[j]
8.   total[j] = total[j] + 1
9.   dealer[j] = dealer[j] ∪ {k}
10.   iteration = iteration + 1

3 Experiment

3.1 Dataset Description

The data required for the experimental analysis were provided by a well-known tobacco and alcohol agent in central Taiwan for the purpose of the case study. The tobacco and alcohol dealer has more than 2,000 dealers, and there are more than 40 trucks responsible for the daily delivery work. Excel is used as the data set, as shown in Fig. 1. It consists of six fields, including the customer code, which is the code of all the dealers of the agent; grade, which is divided into different levels according to the size and sales performance of the dealers and represents the number of delivery times in a week; adjust the number of visits. The increase or decrease of orders due to activities or policies related to tobacco and alcohol, so users need to adjust the number of deliveries made by the dealer. If the space is blank, the delivery is made according to the number of times indicated by the level; block, the more than 2,000 dealers are divided into several sub-blocks, such as A, B, C, D, etc., each block has about more than 200 dealers; finally, the latitude and longitude are needed to calculate the shortest distance between dealers during grouping and to present them on a map after execution, so latitude and longitude need to be calculated and marked on the map. The system designed by this study was implemented in block to verify the vehicle allocation system. The experimental group was used as the system of this study, while the tobacco and alcohol agents manually arranged as the control group manually, and the experimental group is compared and analyzed with the control group.

In the proposed system, a wide range of delivery data is collected through RFID signals. The information acquired includes:

Dealer ID	Ranking	Number of visits	Spatial Area Location	Lngitude	Latitude
020033	Level1	3	A	120.960597	23.949971
020034	Level1	2	A	120.970005	23.964220
020042	Level1	2	A	120.980202	23.940583
020043	Level2	0	A	120.973451	23.957343
020046	Level1	0	A	120.973359	23.960298
020048	Level1	0	A	120.974125	23.967521
020052	Level1	1	B	121.077550	23.945799
020053	Level1	2	A	120.973029	23.959153
020057	Level1	3	A	120.973262	23.957505
020058	Level1	1	B	121.077646	23.945879
020059	Level2	1	A	120.989970	23.907736
020060	Level1	0	A	121.038958	23.997394
020061	Level1	3	C	120.973454	23.957336
020062	Level1	0	C	120.973962	23.965100
020069	Level1	2	A	120.977361	23.959031
020076	Level1	0	A	120.973621	23.956935
020077	Level1	1	A	120.973262	23.957505
020080	Level3	2	A	120.974022	23.965132
020081	Level1	1	A	121.105071	23.967832
020084	Level1	3	A	120.965437	23.963527

Fig. 1. Part of the experimental data

1. Dealer Location: The GPS coordinates (longitude and latitude) of each dealer are gathered.
2. Spatial Area Location: GPS positioning is employed to dynamically cluster different dealer areas.
3. Dealer ID: This unique identifier is used for each dealer.
4. Dealer Ranking: The dealers are categorized into four ranks based on their operational scale and sales performance. The ranks are: Level 1, Level 2, Level 3, and Level 4. The frequency of product delivery to these ranks is as follows: 1 delivery for Level 1, 3 deliveries for Level 2, 2 deliveries for Level 3, and 1 delivery for Level 4.

3.2 Experiment Setting

In this study, the data of block A were tested and the list of dealers who was scheduled to deliver daily by the agent was reprogrammed for vehicle allocation. First, two trucks were assigned to deliver the goods in this block. Next, the assumption is based on the dealership ratio originally assigned to the two trucks, and the test program's effectiveness succeeds in simplifying the labor cost and time spent on manual scheduling.

After the data is put into the system for execution, the data obtained is verified to be better than the manual method by the following steps:

Step 1: The two groups of dealers are counted separately and take the average of the sum of longitude, which is called the average of longitude (Avg_{long}). It is expressed by formula (1). $longitude_i$ represents the longitude of the ith dealer, and the latitude is also averaged by summation of latitude (Avg_{lat}), which is expressed in the way of formula (2), $latitude_i$ represents the latitude of the ith dealer.

$$Avg_{long} = \frac{\sum_{i=1}^{n} longitude_i}{n} \tag{1}$$

$$Avg_{lat} = \frac{\sum_{i=1}^{n} latitude_i}{n} \qquad (2)$$

Step 2: Next, each dealer is averaged with the latitude and longitude into the formula (3). The straight-line distance between $(longitude_i, latitude_i)$ and (Avg_{long}, Avg_{lat}), where $(longitude_i, latitude_i)$ is the longitude and latitude of the ith dealer.

$$
\begin{aligned}
d_i = 6371 &\times arcos[cos(Avg_{lat}) \times cos(latitude_i) \\
&\times cos(Avg_{long} - longitude_i) + sin(Avg_{lat}) \\
&\times sin(latitude_i)]
\end{aligned} \qquad (3)
$$

Step 3: The dealers of the two trucks are respectively calculated by the above formula (3) and then summed up, which is represented by the symbol of sum_{car_j}, , refer to (4).

$$sum_{car_j} = \sum_{i=1}^{n} d_i \qquad (4)$$

Step 4: Finally, add up the sum_{car_j} values of each truck to the formula (5), N_c represents the number of trucks. In other words, it's divided into N_c groups. A smaller value indicates that each group is more concentrated. Relatively, the dealership arranged for the same truck is closer. On the contrary, When the value is higher, it means that the dealers are more dispersed, and the distance between dealers is longer.

$$\sum_{j-1}^{N_c} sum_{car_j} \qquad (5)$$

3.3 Results and Discussion

The results are shown in Table 1 and Fig. 2. In the table, the blue bottom is the result produced by the system. The vehicle allocation of manual method is substituted into formula (6), and the average distance is 117.88. The average distance of the program results is 114.37, 114.37 is less than 117.88, indicating that the distance between dealers in the weekly implementation of the system is relatively close and concentrated. It can be clearly understood that in the total of 6 groups of data from Monday to Saturday, the results of 4 cases of data are respectively that Tuesday, Wednesday, Friday and Saturday are better than manual allocation. Since this problem is an NP-hard problem, the remaining two pieces of data (Monday and Thursday) will be manually adjusted after execution to achieve better results. It takes a lot of time for the salesmen to allocate dealers based on their years of experience. When there is personnel transfer, the employees need to retrain and accumulate experience before they can clearly understand how to arrange the dealers. Through this study, it only takes 425 s to complete the assignment of the dealers, which can not only greatly reduce the time and labor costs, but also enable the business personnel to deal with the shipping related affairs more quickly.

$$\frac{\sum_{w=1}^{6} \sum_{j=1}^{N_c} sum_{car_j}}{6} \qquad (6)$$

Table 1. Comparison of system and manual results in block A.

			The first truck sum_{car_1}	The second truck sum_{car_2}	$\sum_{j=1}^{N_c} sum_{car_j}$
block A	W1	Current Routes	37.77	47.19	**84.96**
		Program Results	45.74	42.04	87.77
	W2	Current Routes	26.38	30.03	56.41
		Program Results	24.07	26.93	**51.01**
	W3	Current Routes	191.76	84.50	276.26
		Program Results	158.74	102.76	**261.50**
	W4	Current Routes	38.46	50.40	**88.86**
		Program Results	46.61	44.90	91.51
	W5	Current Routes	25.76	27.27	53.03
		Program Results	27.68	20.53	**48.21**
	W6	Current Routes	18.38	129.39	147.77
		Program Results	16.72	129.51	**146.23**

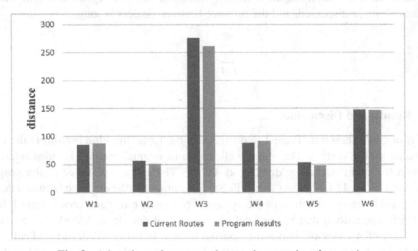

Fig. 2. A bar chart of system and manual comparison in area A

Statistical analysis revealed that the average total mileage from Monday to Saturday, under the existing planning, is 117.88 km. Conversely, the average total for the program-planned route amounted to 114.37 km, marking a reduction of 2.98%. Wednesday (W3) had the highest total mileage, with the most significant difference between the two strategies being 14.76 km.

Knowledge Accumulation for Task Allocation: The current logistical landscape heavily relies on manually acquired experience, which takes a significant amount of time to cultivate, often resulting in organizations having only a single experienced employee. Further compounding this issue is the societal shift towards smaller families, which gradually reduces the availability of apprentices - Factors that all contribute to an impending knowledge gap. However, our method has demonstrated an ability to deliver similar results or even improve efficiency by 2.98%. It facilitates the planning of complex logistical routes and lays the groundwork for the digitization of logistical knowledge.

Rapid Adjustment to Temporary Changes in Order: In the past, when manual task allocation was in place, any sudden change in distributor demands or inventory shortages required substantial time to readjust the routes, which could even cause significant disruption to the scheduling. Therefore, the implementation of our method allows for real-time adjustments of delivery orders and inventory, thereby enhancing the adaptive capacity of the delivery system.

4 Conclusions

In this study, we propose a novel cluster-based optimization method for delivery networks. Utilizing data provided by a renowned tobacco and alcohol distributor in central Taiwan, we implement shipment scheduling and route optimization. The effectiveness of the proposed algorithm is subsequently validated through comparison with preceding manual methods. Notably, the results indicate an improvement of 2.98% over the current procedures, thereby demonstrating the efficacy of the proposed algorithm.

This method aids in distributing to numerous, dispersed, and complex locations on the map, enabling balanced delivery to each location and creating shorter delivery paths. This ultimately reduces order processing times. COMDN can be applied in a wide array of multi-objective delivery and logistics scenarios.

Funding. This research was funded by Department of Industrial Technology, Ministry of Economic Affairs of the Republic of China grant number 112-EC-17-A-25-1243.

References

1. Li, B., Song, G.: Computational logistics for container terminal logistics hubs based on computational lens and computing principles. IEEE Access. **8**, 194820–194835 (2020). https://doi.org/10.1109/access.2020.3033849
2. Cao, Q., et al.: DDQN path planning for unmanned aerial underwater vehicle (UAUV) in underwater acoustic sensor network. Wirel. Netw. (2023). https://doi.org/10.1007/s11276-023-03300-0
3. Park, Y.-B.: A hybrid genetic algorithm for the vehicle scheduling problem with due times and time deadlines. Int. J. Prod. Econ. **73**(2), 175–188 (2001)
4. Yürek, E.E., Özmutlu, H.C.: A decomposition-based iterative optimization algorithm for traveling salesman problem with drone. Trans. Res. Part C: Emerg. Technol. **91**, 249–262 (2018)
5. Yao, B., et al.: An improved particle swarm optimization for carton heterogeneous vehicle routing problem with a collection depot. Ann. Oper. Res. **242**(2), 303–320 (2016). https://doi.org/10.1007/s10479-015-1792-x

6. Yao, B., et al.: Improved artificial bee colony algorithm for vehicle routing problem with time windows. PLoS One. **12**(9), e0181275 (2017). https://doi.org/10.1371/journal.pone.0181275
7. Yu, S., et al.: An improved artificial bee colony algorithm for vehicle routing problem with time windows: A real case in Dalian. Mech. Eng. **8**(8), 1–9 (2016)
8. Zhang, Z., et al.: Research on bi-level optimized operation strategy of micro grid cluster based on IABC algorithm. IEEE Access. **9**, 15520–15529 (2021). https://doi.org/10.1109/access.2021.3053122
9. Wang, Z., et al.: A joint and dynamic routing approach to connected vehicles via LEO constellation satellite networks. Wirel. Netw. (2021). https://doi.org/10.1007/s11276-021-02712-0
10. Mufid, M.R., et al.: Estimated vehicle fuel calculation based on Google map realtime distance. In: 2019 International Electronics Symposium (IES). IEEE (2019)

A Hybrid Deep Learning Approach for Early Detection of Chronic Obstructive Pulmonary Disease

Lun-Ping Hung[1]($\boxtimes$), Hsiang-Tsung Yeh[1], Zong-Jie Wu[2], and Chien-Liang Chen[3]

[1] Department of Information Management, National Taipei University of Nursing and Health Sciences, Taipei 112, Taiwan
lunping@ntunhs.edu.tw
[2] Department of Industrial Engineering and Management, National Yang Ming Chiao Tung University, Hsinchu 300, Taiwan
[3] Department of Innovative Living Design, Overseas Chinese University, Taichung 40721, Taiwan

Abstract. Chronic obstructive pulmonary disease (COPD) is currently the third leading cause of death worldwide. Early detection can help treat the disease and delay its progression. However, chronic diseases are difficult to detect and symptoms often have to develop into severe conditions before they become apparent. Currently, physicians use artificial auscultation as a preliminary means of diagnosing COPD. By detecting the respiratory acoustic phenomena and analyzing the pathology knowledge of patients, physicians can infer and analyze the disease. However, this method still has the possibility of misjudgment or delayed treatment. Therefore, this study uses the ICBIII Respiratory Sound Database Dataset as the basis for analysis data set under the deep learning technology with convolutional neural network models, we classify the features of lung sounds and hope to construct an identification tool that assists in diagnosing COPD. In addition to reducing the time cost of traditional auscultation with this auxiliary tool, after evaluating the model's effectiveness with confusion matrix and accuracy evaluation, we especially estimate its correctness and practical applicability. In the future, it can be recommended for clinical diagnosis and development of an auxiliary diagnosis tool that helps provide early diagnosis of COPD.

Keywords: Deep Learning · Chronic Obstructive Pulmonary Disease · Auxiliary Diagnosis

1 Introduction

Particulate matter (PM) in air pollution is a major factor causing harm to the human body and is also one of the indicators used to assess the level of pollution. When the particle size of suspended matter is equal to or less than 10 μm, it is referred to as PM10. Particles with a size of equal to or less than 2.5 μm are known as fine particulate matter (PM2.5) [1]. Their main components include sulfates, nitrates, ammonia, sodium

D.-J. Deng and J.-C. Chen (Eds.): SGIoT 2023, LNICST 557, pp. 113–121, 2024.
https://doi.org/10.1007/978-3-031-55976-1_11

chloride, black carbon, mineral dust, and water. They also include organic and inorganic complex mixtures suspended in the air [2]. The size of particulate matter determines the final deposition location after inhalation, and PM2.5 can even reach deeper respiratory organs, interfering with gas exchange in the lungs. When the 24-h average concentration of PM2.5 exceeds 35 μg/m^3, it poses a risk to sensitive individuals, such as the elderly, children, and patients with respiratory diseases. If it exceeds 65 μg/m^3, it can harm the health of the general population. According to the World Health Organization, common diseases leading to death due to air pollution include cardiovascular diseases, chronic obstructive pulmonary disease, and cancer [3].

Chronic Obstructive Pulmonary Disease (COPD) is the third leading cause of death worldwide due to diseases. Early detection of COPD is crucial as it allows for timely intervention and the ability to slow down disease progression. The longer COPD remains undetected and untreated, the more severe the impact on lung function becomes. Once lung function is compromised, it can lead to complications such as cardiovascular diseases and respiratory failure, accelerating the time to death. This is why COPD is often referred to as the "silent killer of the lungs."

Due to the chronic nature of Chronic Obstructive Pulmonary Disease (COPD), it is often challenging to detect symptoms in daily life. The respiratory system, which is essential for human survival, serves as the medium through which COPD develops. This means that anyone can unknowingly develop COPD. By the time noticeable symptoms appear, irreversible damage may have already been done to the body. Dealing with such a large number of patients seeking medical attention for COPD puts an immeasurable burden and pressure on the healthcare system, leading to significant costs and strain on medical resources.

Indeed, auscultation is the primary method for the initial diagnosis of respiratory diseases. However, it is a subjective and highly variable diagnostic approach. It requires sensitive perception and extensive experience from skilled physicians who can combine the identification of specific acoustic phenomena with their medical knowledge to accurately diagnose the disease and determine the appropriate treatment methods. The reliance on the expertise of experienced professionals makes it difficult to standardize the process and can lead to variability in diagnoses among different practitioners. As a result, there is a need for additional tools and technologies to complement auscultation and improve the accuracy and efficiency of diagnosing respiratory conditions such as COPD.

Professional diagnosis of respiratory diseases involves several diagnostic processes, such as spirometry, lung volume measurement, and bronchodilator response testing. Spirometry is used to measure the volume and flow rate of air exhaled from the lungs during maximal inhalation. Combined with the mMRC scale and CAT scale analysis, it helps classify patients into four levels and determines appropriate follow-up procedures for each level. Lung volume measurement is essential for assessing total lung capacity and residual lung volume, enabling the differentiation between obstructive and restrictive diseases. If asthma symptoms are present, bronchodilator response testing is conducted to compare the changes before and after the administration of a bronchodilator spray. Significant improvements in airway obstruction after treatment indicate asthma, while the absence of such improvements may suggest Chronic Obstructive Pulmonary Disease (COPD) [4].

The complex and time-consuming nature of these professional diagnostic processes can take anywhere from 10 to 30 min, and with a high volume of patients seeking medical attention, the time and manpower costs can become overwhelming. This research aims to provide physicians with preliminary assistance in identifying COPD and to assist the general public in developing their own preliminary awareness and judgment of the disease.

2 Literature Review

2.1 Application of Artificial Intelligence Technology in Chronic Obstructive Pulmonary Disease

Artificial intelligence covers the fields of machine learning and deep learning. Some researchers have proposed methods for diagnosing respiratory diseases and many studies related to remote healthcare applications have emerged. Priyanka Choudhury et al. Used supervised machine learning algorithms to distinguish between asthma and chronic obstructive pulmonary disease (COPD) by training models with data from multiple interleukins in blood tests [5]. Dat Tran-Anh et al. Combined the Internet of Things with deep learning to create wearable devices that collect respiratory sounds through the mouth. They used a deep learning model based on the SincNet convolutional neural network to classify deep breathing, heavy breathing (respiratory distress), and normal breathing [6]. Binson V.A. et al. Developed an electronic nose detection system, primarily using integrated machine learning algorithms to analyze volatile organic compounds in exhalations to classify COPD, lung cancer, and health. They validated the results using confusion matrices and performance metrics such as accuracy, sensitivity, and specificity [7].

Due to chronic obstructive pulmonary disease-causing airway obstruction, abnormal respiratory sounds such as wheezing and crackles can be detected through auscultation during the breathing process. Many studies focusing on respiratory sound analysis have emerged, Nishi Shahnaj Haider et al. Classifying asthma, chronic obstructive pulmonary disease, and healthy individuals. They utilize wavelet transformation to extract acoustic features and compare the classification results of four machine learning algorithms using a confusion matrix and accuracy, sensitivity, and specificity metrics [8]. Paweł Stasiakiewicz et al. Use wavelet transformation as acoustic features and employ the support vector machine (SVM) algorithm for classification to differentiate pneumonia, pulmonary fibrosis, heart failure, and chronic obstructive pulmonary disease based on sonorous data, Finally, they evaluate the model results based on accuracy, sensitivity, and specificity indicators [9]. Murat Aykanat et al. Utilized Mel frequency cepstral coefficients as acoustic features and spectrograms as image features to classify different respiratory conditions based on lung sound data. The classification results of Support Vector Machine (SVM) and Convolutional Neural Network (CNN) models were evaluated using accuracy, recall, sensitivity, and specificity [10].

2.2 Deep Learning

Deep Learning (DL), one of the methods of artificial intelligence and a branch of machine learning, was proposed by K. Fukushima in 1980 [11]. Its algorithm is based on neural network models inspired by the human brain. In this model, neurons in the human brain are analogous to nodes in computer calculations, and the connections between neurons are analogous to the weights between nodes. The architecture mimics human sensory input, training logic, and classification results, with input layers, hidden layers, and output layers. The most significant difference from traditional machine learning is its ability to effectively handle unstructured data, such as language sentences, images, sounds, and more. Unstructured data implies diverse content, and deep learning can provide the model with multidimensional input data from various perspectives to improve classification performance [12]. Additionally, in deep learning, transfer learning allows for dynamic updates of classifiers, eliminating the need to incur additional time and cost when incorporating new data.

2.3 Acoustic Features

The extraction of acoustic features is a crucial step in acoustic recognition, involving the analysis of sound amplitude signals. Mel-scale Frequency Cepstral Coefficients (MFCC) is a common method for acoustic feature extraction. Human hearing is less sensitive to high frequencies, and MFCC calculations take advantage of this characteristic by using Mel-scale filter banks that approximate the human ear's equal-loudness frequency response. These filters transform the signal into appropriately sized acoustic features. The process begins with initial audio preprocessing, followed by a fast Fourier transform to convert the time-domain signal into the frequency-domain signal. Subsequently, a series of mathematical formulae compress and transform the data into acoustic features that represent the corresponding audio segment [13]. Mel Frequency Cepstral Coefficients (MFCC) Framework Flowchart, as shown in Fig. 1:

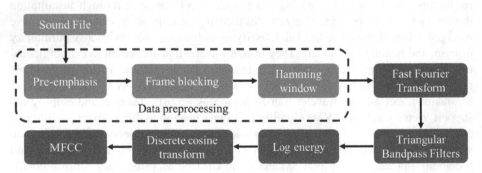

Fig. 1. MFCC Framework Flowchart

Pre-emphasis is the process of passing an audio signal through a high-pass filter. Its purpose is to eliminate noise from vocal cords and lips during the speech production process, primarily emphasizing the resonance peaks in the high-frequency range. Frame blocking involves grouping several sample points into a single observation unit. The Hamming window multiplies each audio frame to enhance the continuity at the left and right ends of the frame. Because it's not easy to observe the characteristics of a sound signal in the time domain, the Fast Fourier Transform (FFT) is used to transform it into the frequency domain to examine the energy distribution. Different energy distributions can represent different sound characteristics. The transformed spectral energy is multiplied by a set of 20 triangular bandpass filters to compute the logarithmic energy output of each filter, which represents the energy of a frame and is an important feature of speech. The logarithmic energy, known as log energy, is the volume of a frame and a crucial feature of speech. The 20 log energy values are then used in the Discrete Cosine Transform (DCT) to calculate the Nth-order Mel Frequency Cepstral Coefficients (MFCCs), with N being a user-selectable parameter. Finally, in practical speech recognition applications, delta cepstral coefficients are often added to show how the MFCCs change over time, resulting in Mel Cepstral coefficients.

The Continuous Wavelet Transform (CWT) is also a tool for acoustic analysis. Its core functionality involves providing different lengths of Hamming window scales based on different frequencies. The calculation is based on translation parameters and scale parameters, and it calculates the continuous wavelet transform parameters according to a user-defined number of frequencies, as show in Fig. 2. This study will apply the two aforementioned acoustic feature extraction methods to the recognition model dataset.

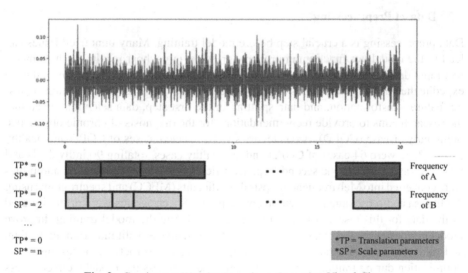

Fig. 2. Continuous Wavelet Transform Operation Visual Chart

3 Method

3.1 Dataset

In this study, the dataset utilizes respiratory sound data provided by the International Conference on Biomedical and Health Informatics (ICBHI). This data was collected by two different research teams from two different countries. The majority of the data was collected in collaboration between the Health Technology Institute of the University of Aveiro and Infante D. Pedro Hospital in Portugal. The remaining portion of the dataset was collected through a collaborative effort involving Aristotle University of Thessaloniki, University of Coimbra, Papanikolaou General Hospital, and Imathia General Hospital in Greece. The dataset encompasses various types of content, including asthma, bronchiectasis, bronchitis, chronic obstructive pulmonary disease, pneumonia, upper respiratory tract infections, lower respiratory tract infections, and healthy cases. Data was collected from seven different anatomical locations, including the front chest on both sides, back on both sides, sides of the body, and the trachea. The data was recorded using a variety of recording equipment, including lapel-style capacitive microphones, traditional stethoscopes, and two electronic stethoscopes, in order to simulate real-world conditions more accurately. The dataset comprises a total of 126 participants and 920 audio files in the WAV format [14].

3.2 Dataset Preprocessing

Data preprocessing is a crucial step before model training. Many unnoticed issues can lead to the model not functioning properly or achieving subpar results, such as incorrect input data or missing values. To ensure the smooth training of the model and even expedite the training process, this stage is divided into three steps: data selection, acoustic feature transformation, and data splitting.In the first step, data selection, given that the research aims to provide recommendations for the diagnosis of chronic obstructive pulmonary disease (COPD), two categories were selected: cases of COPD and healthy cases. There were 64 cases of COPD and 26 healthy cases, totaling 90 individuals and 828 WAV audio files.In the second step, acoustic feature transformation, all audio files were converted into Mel-frequency cepstral coefficients (MFCC) and spectrograms using the librosa audio package in a Python environment. Spectrograms were primarily used as the data for this research's model.Finally, to facilitate the model training, improve model performance, and evaluate model results, the data was split into training, testing, and validation sets. The training set was used for model construction, the testing set for optimization during training, and the validation set to assess the model's effectiveness after construction. The data was initially divided into a 90% training and testing set and a 10% validation set. Within the 90% training and testing set, an 80% training set and a 20% testing set were further split.

3.3 Analysis Model

This study will use the convolutional neural network SincNet mentioned in the literature as the foundation for constructing the training model. We will adjust certain internal parameters based on the aforementioned pre-processed dataset and proceed with the training of the COPD recognition model.

Create a simple one-dimensional CNN model from scratch. By observing that the first data point has 193 parameters, the input layer is set to (193, 1). There are 7 hidden layers, all using the ReLU activation function. The final fully connected layer uses the sigmoid function, suitable for binary classification output. The loss function used is also appropriate for binary classification, binary_crossentropy. Figure 3 shows the model design source code.

```
model = Sequential()
model.add(Conv1D(64, kernel_size=5, activation='relu', input_shape=(193, 1)))

model.add(Conv1D(128, kernel_size=5, activation='relu'))
model.add(MaxPooling1D(2))

model.add(Conv1D(256, kernel_size=5, activation='relu'))

model.add(Dropout(0.3))
model.add(Flatten())

model.add(Dense(512, activation='relu'))
model.add(Dense(2, activation='sigmoid'))

model.compile(loss='binary_crossentropy', optimizer='adam', metrics=['accuracy'])
```

Fig. 3. One-dimensional CNN Model Building Code

3.4 Predictive Assessment

To understand if any unexpected anomalies occur during the model training process, one can observe the changes in model accuracy and loss values to identify issues with the training and test sets. Ideally, as the model's accuracy increases, the loss values decrease. However, it is also possible to encounter situations of overfitting and underfitting. When overfitting occurs, it means that the model performs very well on the training data, resulting in low loss values, but it performs poorly during testing, leading to low accuracy. In the case of underfitting, the model exhibits poorer performance on the training data.

To ensure the feasibility of the diagnostic recommendations provided, this study will utilize a validation set to evaluate the model's performance by calculating metrics in the form of a Confusion Matrix:

- TP (true positive): Actual cases of COPD correctly identified as COPD.
- TN (true negative): Actual cases without COPD correctly identified as non-COPD.
- FP (false positive): Actual cases with COPD incorrectly identified as non-COPD.
- FN (false negative): Actual cases without COPD incorrectly identified as COPD.

Using these metrics from the Confusion Matrix, the following indicator can be calculated:

Accuracy is the ratio of correctly classified samples in the validation dataset to the total number of samples, and it can serve as a comprehensive performance score for the model.

4   Conclusion

Currently, a complete dataset has been obtained and two categories, COPD and healthy, have been selected. Data preprocessing has also been completed, with audio files transformed into Mel-frequency cepstral coefficient (MFCC) features. Successful experiments in building recognition models on this dataset using methods from other domains have been conducted, verifying the feasibility of using this dataset in our research. From Fig. 4, it can be observed that the trained model's recognition results, with the SincNet model and data preprocessing settings, exhibit good recognition performance.

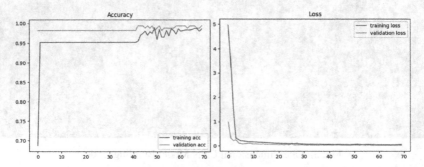

Fig. 4. Training process of a one-dimensional CNN model

5   Discussion

This study utilized the aforementioned publicly available dataset and, through data preprocessing and model development, achieved promising initial results. It is our hope that this research can provide recommendations for predicting the presence of chronic obstructive pulmonary disease (COPD) based on acoustic respiratory features, offering objective diagnostic suggestions for healthcare professionals in the future. We also intend to incorporate other models to assess their effectiveness and feasibility while exploring the relevant features of COPD with input from other researchers and expert physicians. This will enable the construction of a more precise and effective convolutional neural network model for deep learning, which can be used to provide valuable predictions and guidance for COPD.

References

1. Health Promotion Administration-Ministry of Health and Welfare. Air pollution health self-protection area (2022). Available from: https://www.hpa.gov.tw/pages/list.aspx?nodeid=441

2. World Health Organization: Ambient (outdoor) air pollution (2022). Available from: https://www.who.int/news-room/fact-sheets/detail/ambient-(outdoor)-air-quality-and-health

3. World Health Organization: 7 million premature deaths annually linked to air pollution (2014). Available from: https://www.who.int/news/item/25-03-2014-7-million-premature-deaths-annually-linked-to-air-pollution

4. Taichung Hospital-Ministry of Health and Welfare: Pulmonary function tests; Available from: https://www.taic.mohw.gov.tw/?aid=52&pid=60&page_name=detail&iid=243

5. Choudhury, P., Biswas, S., Singh, G., Pal, A., Ghosh, N., Ojha, A.K.: Chaudhury, K, Immunological profiling and development of a sensing device for detection of IL-13 in COPD and asthma. Bioelectrochemistry **143**, 107971 (2022)

6. Tran-Anh, D., Vu, N.H., Nguyen-Trong, K., Pham, C.: Multi-task learning neural networks for breath sound detection and classification in pervasive healthcare. Pervasive and Mobile Computing **86**, 101685 (2022)

7. Binson, V.A., Subramoniam, M., Mathew, L.: Detection of COPD and Lung Cancer with electronic nose using ensemble learning methods. Clinical Chimica Acta **523**, 231–238 (2021)

8. Haider, N.S., Behera, A.K.: Computerized lung sound based classification of asthma and chronic obstructive pulmonary disease (COPD). Biocybernetics and Biomedical Engineering **42**(1), 42–59 (2022)

9. Stasiakiewicz, P., et al.: Automatic classification of normal and sick patients with crackles using wavelet packet decomposition and support vector machine. Biomed. Signal Process. Control **67**, 102521 (2021)

10. Aykanat, M., Kılıç, Ö., Kurt, B., Saryal, S.: Classification of lung sounds using convolutional neural networks. EURASIP Journal on Image and Video Processing **1**, 65 (2017)

11. Fukushima, K.: Neocognitron: A self-organizing neural network model for a mechanism of pattern recognition unaffected by shift in position. Biological Cybernetics **36**, 193–202 (1980)

12. Parashar, A., Parashar, A., Ding, W., Shabaz, M., Rida, I.: Data preprocessing and feature selection techniques in gait recognition: A comparative study of machine learning and deep learning approaches. Pattern Recogn. Lett. **172**, 65–73 (2023)

13. Nishikawa, K., Akihiro, K., Hirakawa, R., Kawano, H., Nakatoh, Y.: Machine learning model for discrimination of mild dementia patients using acoustic features. Cognitive Robotics **2**, 21–29 (2022)

14. ICBHI Respiratory Sound Database; Available from: https://bhichallenge.med.auth.gr/ICBHI_2017_Challenge

Predicting Teaching Effectiveness Base on Technology Integrated Language Learning

Wan-Chi Yang[1], Yi-Ti Lin[2], Po-Li Chen[3], and Huan-Chao Keh[4](✉)

[1] General Education Center, National Taipei University of Nursing and Health Sciences, Taipei, Taiwan
wanchi@ntunhs.edu.tw
[2] Department of English, Tamkang University, New Taipei City, Taiwan
ytlin@mail.tku.edu.tw
[3] Department of Psychology and Counseling, National Taipei University of Education, Taipei, Taiwan
henry1chen@mail.ntue.edu.tw
[4] Department of Computer Science and Information Engineering, Tamkang University, New Taipei City, Taiwan
hckeh@mail.tku.edu.tw

Abstract. This research explores the link between English teachers' acceptance of Instant Response Systems (IRSs) and their perceived teaching effectiveness. The study involved 151 English teachers who completed an online survey and participated in semi-structured interviews about their IRS acceptance and perceived teaching effectiveness. The findings reveal that teaching effectiveness is positively influenced by constructivist pedagogical beliefs, attitude toward IRS use, perceived IRS usefulness, and facilitating conditions. The integration of IRS-based tools has demonstrated benefits such as increased student motivation, engagement, and achievement. These tools also invigorate classroom dynamics and provide timely feedback, thereby enhancing teachers' ability to assess student learning progress.

Keywords: Teaching Effectiveness · Information Communication Technology Integration · Instant Response Systems

1 Introduction

Educators' adoption of information communication technologies (ICTs) has been widely discussed in recent decades. Numerous studies have applied the TAM (Technology Acceptance Model) [10, 11] and UTAUT (Unified Theory of Technology Acceptance and Use of Technology) [21] models to investigate teachers' intentions to use technology in teaching. These frameworks have identified multiple influencing factors [1, 3, 13, 15, 16].

D.-J. Deng and J.-C. Chen (Eds.): SGIoT 2023, LNICST 557, pp. 122–129, 2024.
https://doi.org/10.1007/978-3-031-55976-1_12

Digital tools such as Instant Response Systems (IRSs) are commonly employed to facilitate effective classroom practices [2, 12]. IRS tools assist teachers in identifying knowledge gaps during instruction, enabling them to make necessary pedagogical adjustments to achieve their teaching objectives. Unlike previous studies that aimed to identify the influence of various factors on teachers' intentions to use technology, the current research not only considers pedagogical beliefs but also examines constructivist pedagogical beliefs alongside other technology acceptance factors. The study investigates the connections between teachers' acceptance of IRS and their teaching effectiveness. Additionally, it explores teachers' perceptions and attitudes regarding the use of IRS in language instruction.

2 Related Work

2.1 Teaching Effectiveness

Research indicates that teaching practices significantly impact students' motivation and learning outcomes [9, 20] with effective teaching enhancing the likelihood of achieving desired goals.

Calaguas (2012) conducted a literature review spanning 2000 to 2009, identifying six dimensions of teaching effectiveness: personality, subject matter expertise, relational competence with students, professional competence, teaching style, and classroom management. This research underscores the complexity of teaching effectiveness, which encompasses multiple dimensions. Recognizing that each teacher possesses a unique teaching style, self-evaluation has been suggested as a valuable tool for teachers to gain insights into their teaching practices. It enables teachers to assess their strengths and weaknesses and discover avenues for enhancing their effectiveness [5].

Buela and Joseph (2015) investigated how high school teachers' personalities relate to their self-evaluated teaching effectiveness. Teaching effectiveness was gauged across multiple dimensions, including classroom management, preparation, subject knowledge, interpersonal skills, and teacher attributes. They discovered a noteworthy link between extraverted personalities and proficiency in subject knowledge.

Similarly, Motallebzadeh et al. (2018) examined the connection between EFL (English as a Foreign Language) teachers' reflective practices and their perceived teaching effectiveness. Their findings showed a positive and substantial correlation between overall reflective practices and teaching effectiveness.

These studies underscore the multi-dimensional nature of teaching effectiveness, influenced by various factors. Some teacher-related attributes, like teaching style, personality traits, and reflective abilities, can best be assessed by the teacher themselves. As a result, the current research employs self-evaluation to measure teaching effectiveness.

2.2 Factoring Affecting Teachers' Intentions to Adopt Technology

The TAM and UTAUT models are built on certain assumptions. They posit that individuals' actual use of information technology is reflected in their intentions to use the technology, and their reactions to using technology impact these intentions [21]. Among the two models, reactions to information technology use are represented by core variables.

In TAM, core variables include perceived usefulness (PU), perceived ease of use (PEU), and attitude toward using (ATU). UTAUT, on the other hand, includes performance expectancy, effort expectancy, social factors (SF), and facilitating conditions (FC) as core variables. Notably, some of these core variables share conceptual similarities. For instance, perceived ease of use aligns with effort expectancy, while perceived usefulness corresponds to performance expectancy.

Previous research has highlighted that computer self-efficacy (CSE) plays a significant role in shaping PU and PEU for teachers [13, 17]. CSE not only mediates the relationship between perceived usefulness and perceived ease of use for teachers but also influences students' learning behaviors related to technology use [14].

Constructivist pedagogical beliefs (CPB) also contribute to PU and PEU. Teachers who embrace CPB prioritize encouraging students to construct meaning independently [4]. Studies have shown that EFL teachers' CPB significantly influence their perceptions of usefulness and ease of use [15]. Additionally, adopting constructivist-oriented teaching practices leads to higher perceptions of teaching effectiveness and increased learning satisfaction [20].

The remaining core variables are social factors (SF), facilitating conditions (FC), and attitude toward using (ATU). ATU is influenced by PU and PEU and determines users' intentions to use technology. SF positively impacts PU [17] and significantly affects university teachers' intentions to use technology [1, 16]. FC is a crucial factor influencing teachers' technology usage behaviors [16] and directly affects their intentions to use technology, explaining substantial variation in PEU [3, 17].

3 Methodology

A mixed-method research design was used to answer the following research questions:

(1) What is the relationship between IRS acceptance factors and EFL teachers' perceived teaching effectiveness?
(2) What are the determining factors that influence EFL teachers' perceived teaching effectiveness?
(3) How do EFL teachers perceive the effectiveness of using IRS tools in teaching?

Quantitative data were collected from 151 EFL teachers in Taiwan on their perceptions of IRS in language teaching via a questionnaire. Participants have diverse educational backgrounds and have employed IRS in their teaching environments, which encompass elementary and junior high schools, senior high schools, universities, and language schools. The questionnaire includes three sections. Section one included demographic information. Demographic information contains teachers' personal background, which includes their gender, age, the level of education taught, as well as years of experience teaching and using IRS assessment tools. Section two dealt with the factors related to IRS acceptance. Section three dealt with perceived teaching effectiveness. The measurement of IRS acceptance factors is comprised of 7 domains and 35 items. The measurement of teaching effectiveness includes four aspects and 27 items. The items were validated by previous studies. They were assessed using a 4-point Likert scale, ranging from "strongly disagree" (1) to "strongly agree" (4), with adjustments made to align with the specific context of this study. A semi-structured interview was adopted to probe EFL teachers' attitude, thoughts, and perceptions about the use of IRS in teaching. The interview includes 8 questions, structured around the three key factors (PU, PEU, and ATU) in the TAM model. The questions can be found in Table 1.

Table 1. Interview questions and TAM factors

Questions	TAM
1. How did you decide to use IRS tools?	PU
2. Do you find IRS tools to be useful in your class? If so, why?	PU
3. How do IRS tools impact teaching?	PU
4. How easy is it to use IRS tools while you teach?	PEU
5. How easy is it for you to integrate IRS tools in teaching?	PEU
6. What perceived barriers prevent you from using IRS tools in teaching?	PEU
7. What are your perceptions regarding the use of IRS tools to teach?	ATU
8. What do you like or dislike about using IRS tools in teaching?	ATU

4 Results

4.1 Quantitative Data

A moderate to strong positive correlation was found between most of the independent variables. As for the dependent variable, teaching effectiveness was found to significantly correlate with all independent variables except for PU.

The highest correlation was found between ATU and PEU with a correlation of 0.760 ($p<0.01$), followed by ATU and PU with a correlation of 0.726 ($p<0.01$). These were followed by PEU and CSE with a correlation of 0.701 ($p<0.01$).

However, no significant relationship was found between CPB and SF, CPB and PU, CPB and PEU, CPB and ATU, and PU and TE. CPB only correlated significantly with FC ($r = 0.162$, $p<0.05$), CSE ($r = 0.188$, $p<0.05$), and TE ($r = 0.522$, $p<0.01$) (Table 2).

Table 2. Pearson correlation coefficients for the study variables (n = 151).

Variables	FC	SF	CSE	CPB	PU	PEU	ATU	TE
FC	1							
SF	0.558**	1						
CSE	0.378**	0.300**	1					
CPB	0.162*	0.157	0.188*	1				
PU	0.387**	0.437**	0.592**	0.093	1			
PEU	0.328**	0.189*	0.701**	0.092	0.512**	1		
ATU	0.371**	0.314**	0.695**	0.129	0.726**	0.760**	1	
TE	0.248**	0.169*	0.253**	0.522**	0.082	0.212**	0.245**	1

Note. * Correlation is significant at 0.05 level (2-tailed). ** Correlation is significant at 0.01 level (2-tailed).TE = teaching effectiveness, FC = facilitating conditions, SF = social factors, CSE = computer self-efficacy, CPB = constructivist pedagogical beliefs, PU = perceived usefulness of IRS, PEU = perceived ease of IRS use, ATU = attitude towards IRS use

A stepwise regression analysis was performed to determine the relationships among the variables. The stepwise regression analysis identified four key predictor variables for teaching effectiveness: CPB, ATU, PU, and FC. These variables significantly contribute to the variance in teaching effectiveness. In the initial step, CPB explained 27.2% of the variance. Subsequently, in the second step, ATU contributed an additional 3.2% to the explanation of teaching effectiveness. PU and FC accounted for 1.9% of the variance each in the third and fourth steps, respectively.

Notably, it's worth mentioning that PU exhibited a negative correlation with teaching effectiveness. This could be attributed to the lack of specificity regarding the particular IRS tools referred to in this study. While teachers generally perceive IRS tools as useful, their effectiveness may vary depending on the specific teaching context in which they are applied.

When ranked by their contribution to the variance, CPB emerged as the most influential predictor, followed by ATU, PU, and FC, in that order. Together, these four variables collectively explain approximately 34.2% of the variance in teaching effectiveness (Table 3).

Table 3. Stepwise regression analysis concerning the prediction of teaching effectiveness (n = 151).

Step	Variable	Coefficient	SE	p	t	R^2	VIF
Step 1						0.272	
	CPB	0.522**	0.60	0.000	7.464	0.272	1.000
Step 2						0.304	
	CPB	0.498**	0.60	0.000	7.206	0.272	1.017
	ATU	0.180*	0.036	0.010	2.605	0.032	10.17
Step 3						0.323	
	CPB	0.498**	0.059	0.000	7.279	0.272	10.17
	ATU	0.326*	0.051	0.001	3.287	0.032	2.133
	PU	-0.200*	0.044	0.044	-2.031	0.019	2.116
Step 4						0.342	
	CPB	0.481**	0.059	0.000	7.039	0.272	1.034
	ATU	0.299*	0.051	0.003	3.025	0.032	2.171
	PU	-0.238*	0.045	0.018	-2.397	0.019	2.191
	FC	0.151*	0.036	0.043	2.041	0.019	1.220

Note. ** $p<0.001$, * $p<0.05$

4.2   Qualitative Data: PU, PEU, and ATU

Teachers perceived that IRS tools had a positive impact on learners' motivation and engagement. These tools facilitated real-time assessment of students' comprehension, enabling teachers to promptly adjust their instruction and curriculum to meet students' needs. Some game-based learning platforms incorporated appealing audio and visual effects, enhancing the overall learning experience by making it more dynamic and engaging. Consequently, students became emotionally and cognitively involved in the classroom.

Regarding the perceived ease of using IRS tools, concerns were raised about the functionality of the IRS system, teachers' technical proficiency, and the stability of internet connections. However, the majority of teachers expressed a positive attitude toward IRS-based tools due to their easy accessibility and user-friendly interfaces. Nevertheless, a small number of interviewees had reservations about the functionality of the online platform.

In terms of attitude toward IRS use, all participants welcomed the adoption of this technology. They unanimously agreed that IRS technology had a positive impact on their teaching practices, primarily by helping identify knowledge gaps among students.

5 Discussion

The current study discovered significant correlations between constructivist pedagogical beliefs (CPB), attitude toward IRS use (ATU), facilitating conditions (FC), perceived usefulness of IRS (PU), and teaching effectiveness. CPB emerged as the strongest predictor of teaching effectiveness, followed by ATU, FC, and PU. The study also confirmed the positive association between constructivist pedagogical beliefs and teaching effectiveness. ATU, the second most influential predictor, was positively linked to teaching effectiveness. Additionally, PU proved to be a significant indicator of teaching effectiveness.

Consistent with prior research on IRS (Instant Response System) studies [8, 19], this study underscores the significance of integrating IRS-based tools in teaching. Furthermore, it aligns with [19] perspective by affirming that IRS-based tools strongly influence students' motivation and engagement. The inclusion of audio-visual effects, instant feedback, and gamification elements enhances students' engagement on cognitive, behavioral, and emotional levels, thereby increasing the likelihood that they will retain information as it is genuinely learned.

Despite the evident benefits, EFL teachers face challenges when using IRS tools in their classrooms. These challenges encompass a lack of technical expertise, difficulties in accessing a stable internet connection, and occasional glitches in the online platform, all of which hinder effective classroom implementation.

6 Conclusion

This research explored the impact of facilitating conditions, social factors, computer self-efficacy, constructivist pedagogical beliefs, perceived usefulness of IRS, perceived ease of IRS use, and attitude toward IRS use on teaching effectiveness among EFL teachers in Taiwan. It also delved into teachers' perceptions of the effectiveness of IRS-based tools in teaching.

The findings highlighted that constructivist pedagogical beliefs, attitude toward IRS use, and facilitating conditions positively and significantly influenced teaching effectiveness. In contrast, perceived usefulness of IRS had a significant negative impact.

Moreover, this study provided empirical evidence concerning the influence of IRS-based tools on language learning. Insights from interviews confirmed the driving factors and barriers to the adoption of IRS-based tools in the EFL teaching context. According to teachers' responses, IRS-based tools injected energy into the classroom and offered timely feedback for understanding students' learning progress. These perceptions influenced their teaching practices. Identified barriers to IRS adoption encompassed technical shortcomings, limitations in internet infrastructure, insufficient computer skills, and a related lack of technological knowledge. These factors hindered EFL teachers from effectively integrating IRS-based tools into their classes.

References

1. Abd Rahman, S.F., Md Yunus, M., Hashim, H.: Applying UTAUT in predicting ESL lecturers intention to use flipped learning. Sustainability **12**(15), 8571 (2021)

2. Alawadhi, A., Abu-Ayyash, E.A.S.: Students' perceptions of Kahoot!: an exploratory mixed-method study in EFL undergraduate classrooms in the UAE. Educ. Inf. Technol. **26**, 3629–3658 (2021)
3. Bai, B., Wang, J., Chai, C.-S.: Understanding Hong Kong primary school English teachers' continuance intention to teach with ICT. Comput. Assist. Lang. Learn. 1–23. (2021)
4. Becker, H.J.: Finding from the teaching, learning, and computing survey. Educ. Policy Anal. Arch. **8**, 51 (2000)
5. Berk, R.A.: Survey of 12 strategies to measure teaching effectiveness. Int. J. Teach. Learn. High. Educ. **17**(1), 48–62 (2005)
6. Buela, S., Joseph, M.C.: Relationship between personality and teacher effectiveness of high school teachers. International J. Ind. Psychol. **3**(1) (2015)
7. Calaguas, G.M.: Teacher effectiveness scale in higher education: development and psychometric properties. Int. J. Res. Stud Educ **2**(1) (2012)
8. Cancino, M., Capredoni, R.: Assessing pre-service EFL teachers' perceptions regarding an online student response system. Taiwan J. TESOL **17**(2), 91–118 (2020)
9. Cudney, E.A., Ezzell, J.M.: Evaluating the impact of teaching methods on student motivation. J. STEM Educ. Innov. Res **18**(1), 32–49 (2017)
10. Davis, F.D.: A technology acceptance model for empirically testing new end-user information systems: Theory and results. Doctoral thesis, Massachusetts Institute of Technology. MIT Libraries (1985)
11. Davis, F.D.: Perceived usefulness, perceived ease of use, and user acceptance of information technology. MIS Q. **13**(3), 319 (1989)
12. Eltahir, M.E., Alsalhi, N.R., Al-Qatawneh, S., Alqudah, H.A., Jaradat, M.: The impact of game-based learning (GBL) on students' motivation, engagement and academic performance on an Arabic language grammar course in higher education. Educ. Inf. Technol. **26**, 3251–3278 (2020)
13. Hong, X., Zhang, M., Liu, Q.: Preschool teachers' technology acceptance during the COVID-19: an adapted technology acceptance model. Front. Psychol. **12** (2021)
14. Li, R., Meng, Z., Tian, M., Zhang, Z., Ni, C., Xiao, W.: Examining EFL learners' individual antecedents on the adoption of automated writing evaluation in China. Comput. Assist. Lang. Learn. **32**(7), 784–804 (2019)
15. Liu, H., Lin, C.-H., Zhang, D.: Pedagogical beliefs and attitudes towards information and communication technology: a survey of teachers of English as a foreign language in China. Comput. Assist. Lang. Learn. **30**(8), 745–765 (2017)
16. Ma, M., Chen, J., Zheng, P., Wu, Y.: Factors affecting EFL teachers' affordance transfer of ICT resources in China. Interact. Learn. Environ. **30**(6), 1044–1059 (2019)
17. Mei, B., Brown, G.T., Teo, T.: Toward an understanding of preservice English as a foreign language teachers' acceptance of computer-assisted language learning 2.0 in the People's Republic of China. J. Educ. Comput. Res. **56**(1), 74–104 (2017)
18. Motallebzadeh, K., Ahmadi, F., Hosseinnia, M.: The relationship between EFL teachers' reflective practices and their teaching effectiveness: a structural equation modeling approach. Cogent Psychol. **5**(1), 1424682 (2018)
19. Reynold, E.D., Taylor, B.: Kahoot!: EFL instructors' implementation experiences and impacts on students' vocabulary knowledge. Comput. Assist. Lang. Learn. Electron. J. **21**(2), 70–92 (2020)
20. Tadesse, T., Gillies, R.M., Manathunga, C.: The effect of informal cooperative learning pedagogy on teaching effectiveness, task orientation, and learning satisfaction in undergraduate classrooms in Ethiopia. High. Educ. Res. Dev. **40**(3), 627–645 (2020)
21. Venkatesh, V., Morris, M.G., Davis, G.B., Davis, F.D.: User acceptance of information technology: toward a unified view. MIS Q. **27**(3), 425 (2003)

Complex Industrial Machinery Health Diagnosis Challenges and Strategies

Hsiao-Yu Wang[✉] and Ching-Hua Hung

Department of Mechanical Engineering, National Yang Ming Chiao Tung University, Hsinchu City 300093, Taiwan
shon0808@gmail.com

Abstract. This study is dedicated to addressing a spectrum of pivotal challenges and predicting their potential ramifications. Specifically, its objectives encompass the detection of tool breakage in milling-turning composite machinery, the assessment of the service life of punching machine heads, and the evaluation of mold longevity in forging apparatus, among other intricacies. The overarching objective is the establishment of an equipment health diagnosis system tailored for intricate industrial setups. It is evident from our interactions with the industry that the rationale for monitoring strategies and threshold values are contingent upon the idiosyncratic attributes of the equipment and the sector. While the metal processing sector has been trailing behind the semiconductor industry in the realm of intelligent monitoring by an approximate span of a decade, it faces an analogous array of challenges. These encompass dwindling demographics, leading to an increased reliance on external labor for shifts, elevated personnel turnover rates thereby limiting the availability of experienced personnel for tasks such as tool changes, mold replacements, and maintenance. Additionally, the necessity to uphold traceability standards for mold and punching head usage history, notably in the context of aerospace industry compliance, compounds these challenges. Consequently, the industry aspires to achieve two paramount objectives for vital production equipment: first, the execution of failure diagnostics to appraise tool or mold longevity and assess product quality. Second, the transition from time-based to condition-based maintenance practices, even under conditions that necessitate frequent mold substitutions to cater to diverse product manufacturing needs.

Keywords: Root Mean Square · Statistical overlap factor · Ensemble Empirical Mode Decomposition · Bayesian regularization

1 Introduction

Piercing processes are extensively used in stamping products, often equipped with up to 24 die sets. However, varying levels of wear due to uneven loading, machining tolerances, and assembly factors pose significant challenges. When a die fails, it necessitates the removal of molds for die replacement. Systematically assessing the remaining lifespan of other dies and replacing them simultaneously could reduce production losses

D.-J. Deng and J.-C. Chen (Eds.): SGIoT 2023, LNICST 557, pp. 130–140, 2024.
https://doi.org/10.1007/978-3-031-55976-1_13

during mold changeovers. The theoretical challenges lie in unfavorable signal-to-noise ratios in factory environments, minimal stiffness variations in micro-die structures, and disturbances from rigid body modes in signals, all of which affect failure diagnosis outcomes.

Stamping processes are highly nonlinear transient procedures. Developing knowledge-experience-based solutions often results in non-generic, case-specific monitoring systems. Additionally, the time-consuming process of establishing the learning curve for these monitoring systems is a concern. The research focus of our team includes the proper decoupling of fault characteristics or signals and their selection as indicators of machine health status in low-sample learning scenarios.

2 Materials and Methods

This study focuses on constructing a monitoring system for a C-frame punch press, targeting two main objectives: 1) abnormal machine operation vibration detection, and 2) abnormal detection of tools (such as dies and punch heads) in the stamping process. The monitoring positions planned by our team are illustrated in Fig. 1.

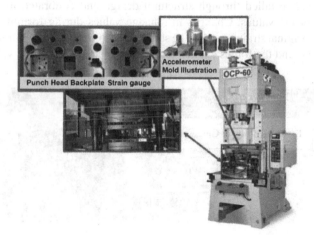

Fig. 1. Sensor Planning Illustration Diagram

An accelerometer device is installed on the crankshaft assembly for long-term monitoring, allowing observation of any misalignment or wear in the crankshaft and bushing. However, for shorter-term monitoring, it is utilized to observe abnormal vibrations in the mold during stamping, providing insights into punch head wear issues. The actual on-site installation is shown in Fig. 2.

Fig. 2. On-Site Sensor Installation Diagram

Another monitoring position involves embedding sensors into the backplate of the mold, as depicted in Fig. 3. The backplate, being a direct force-bearing component in the punch head, serves as an excellent source of signals for studying punch head wear. Strain gauges, replacing costlier load cells, are predominantly used in the backplate. These strain gauges are installed through structural design and calibrated to convert strain signals into tonnage values. Changes in tonnage values during forming are observed concerning the original strain signals. The study has also verified the relationship between punch head wear and the forces exerted on the backplate and machine vibrations.

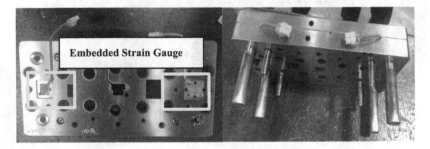

Fig. 3. Post-Installation Configuration Diagram on the Die

The key sensor trigger timing is facilitated by a digital encoder installed on the machine's crankshaft, significantly reducing post-signal processing tasks such as signal stitching and eliminating unnecessary signals. During the initial stages of research, on-site technicians use our designed app to annotate abnormal time points, such as punch head fractures, mold abnormalities, and machine anomalies. This practice narrows down the range for identifying signal differences and accelerates signal labeling until the algorithm effectively extracts identifiable abnormal signals.

The subsequent sections will provide a detailed description of the monitoring system's planning, including hardware (sensors, signal processors, signal extractors, industrial computers) and software (monitoring system platform).

2.1 Hardware Measurement Architecture

The hardware configuration utilizes sensors that provide analog signal output. These analog signals are coupled with a signal conditioner (SC) to provide IEPE (Integrated Electronics Piezoelectric) power to the accelerometers. The signal conditioner also serves to preprocess the signals, including filtering out any power disturbances originating from the factory environment. Subsequently, the analog signals are converted to digital signals using a Data Acquisition (DAQ) system.

For the accelerometers, a 16-bit Analog to Digital Converter (ADC) is employed for data conversion. In the case of strain gauges, a high-specification 24-bit ADC is utilized, enabling precise measurement of metal deformation down to a strain level of $(10)^{-6}$.

The two depicted snapshot cards represent physical signal lines that connect to a Data Acquisition (DAQ) unit, which is then connected to the monitoring system on the computer. The monitoring system is designed to accommodate both wireless Wi-Fi and physical Ethernet network connections, depending on the actual on-site configuration.

In terms of software design, it is customized to meet the specific requirements of Company A. The interface includes a homepage displaying key statistics such as machine utilization rates and the actual number of completed stamping operations. This information is presented in a way that is easily understandable for on-site personnel. The subsequent pages provide real-time reception of the raw signals, allowing our personnel to monitor the status of signal lines and hardware for any anomalies or irregularities.

2.2 Methods

In related research, our team has achieved preliminary results in monitoring the lifespan of single punching heads in the punching process. In the findings presented in [5], it was confirmed that through time analysis and frequency analysis, the extracted feature signals could establish a correlation between punching head wear and burr height. In [6], a logistic regression analysis and the use of the statistical overlap factor were employed to assess the logical thresholds for decision-making in the monitoring system. All of these experimental and analytical research outcomes were conducted using a 50-ton hydraulic punching machine in our university's smart factory.

In terms of software design, it is customized to meet the specific requirements of Company A. The interface includes a homepage displaying key statistics such as machine utilization rates and the actual number of completed stamping operations. This information is presented in a way that is easily understandable for on-site personnel. The subsequent pages provide real-time reception of the raw signals, allowing our personnel to monitor the status of signal lines and hardware for any anomalies or irregularities.

2.3 Process

The signal explanation in Fig. 4 is derived from our team's research on stamping processes and the reference [4]. A complete stamping vibration signal is divided into three phases based on the relative time corresponding to the stamping machine's stroke:

1. Upper Die Pressing Stage: The phase when the upper die presses the material.
2. Punching Stage: The phase when the punch pierces through the material.
3. Upper Die Lifting Stage: The phase when the upper die is lifted.

By conducting statistical comparisons in the referenced study, it was determined that the vibration signal during the punching stage provides more accurate characteristics of the actual stamping process. It was also confirmed that there is a positive correlation between punch wear and the vibration during the punching stage.

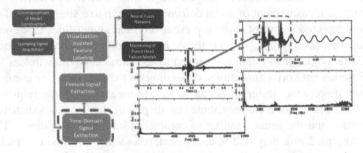

Fig. 4. Research Process Diagram - Time-Domain Signal Extraction

In Fig. 5, an explanation of the measured vibration and strain signals in an actual company B stamping plant is provided. By measuring the z-axis vibration using an accelerometer, the signals during a complete punching process can be divided into four signal amplitudes, corresponding to the following stages:

1. **Bed Movement:** The upper bed moves downward from the top.
2. **Die Pressing Stage:** The vibration signal generated when the pressing plate first contacts the sheet metal and the lower die.
3. **Punching Stage:** The moment when the punch extends downward to pierce the sheet metal.
4. **Lifting Stage:** After the punching is complete, the upper bed moves upward, and the pressing plate disengages from the sheet metal.

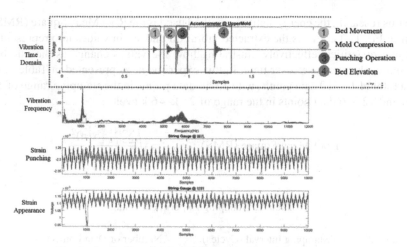

Fig. 5. Time-Domain Signal Extraction Explanation Diagram

Based on the signal extraction process, the third stage, the punching stage, is isolated, as shown in Fig. 6. From top to bottom, the figure displays the punching stage in the time domain vibration, frequency domain vibration, punch strain, and external strain, completing a time-domain extraction process. The following will explain the overall number of experiments and how each punching event is converted into energy values to compare their differences.

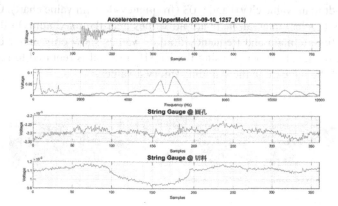

Fig. 6. Time-Domain Signal Extraction - Punching Segment Signal Diagram

Based on the signal extraction process, the third stage, the punching stage, is isolated, as shown in Fig. 6. From top to bottom, the figure displays the punching stage in the time domain vibration, frequency domain vibration, punch strain, and external strain, completing a time-domain extraction process. The following will explain the overall number of experiments and how each punching event is converted into energy values to compare their differences.

In this research, the energy statistics method used is the Root Mean Square (RMS), as shown in Eq. 1. It converts the extracted vibration and strain values into representative numerical quantities, effectively illustrating how the values change as the number of stamping cycles increases over time. In this experiment, as presented in Table 1, there were a total of 15,410 data points, with 3,044 data points in the stamping range of 1–5 k cycles and 12,366 data points in the range of 25 k–46 k cycles.

$$\text{Root Mean Square (RMS)} : x_{rms} = \sqrt{\frac{\sum_{n=1}^{N} x(n)^2}{n}} \tag{1}$$

Table 1. Stamping Experiment Data.

Item Interval	Stamping Interval (Cycles)	Number of Data Points (Entries)
1	1–5 k	3,044
2	25 k–46 k	12,366

Figure 7 consists of upper and lower panels, each displaying the time-domain and frequency-domain vibration signals after extraction. The energy trends, calculated using the RMS method, are also presented. Both sets of data from the two stamping intervals are overlaid for comparison. From these two panels, it can be observed that for the 25 k–46 k (cycles) interval, approximately 50% of the values fall near the maximum values of 0.4 (time-domain value chart) and 0.03 (frequency-domain value chart). Conversely, for the 1–5 k (cycles) interval, there are no values near the maximum. In this context, the original time-domain and frequency-domain values show only minor differences. Further feature signal extraction using the EEMD method is required to represent the magnitude of the increase in the stamping interval values.

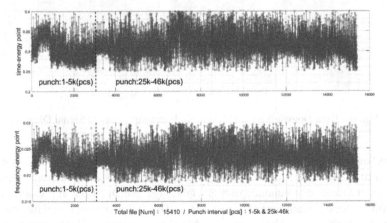

Fig. 7. Illustrates the vibration energy chart, with the upper panel displaying time-domain energy values and the lower panel showing frequency-domain energy values.

Figure 8 depicts the strain signals extracted from the punching and appearance forming processes, with the upper panel showing the strain signal from the punching process and the lower panel displaying the strain signal from the appearance forming process. The strain sensor behind the punch can most directly reflect the stress conditions and wear level of the punch during the punching process. In the upper panel, the strain signal from the punching process exhibits linear growth, increasing from $2.3 * 10^{-3}$ to $2.125 * 10^{-3}$ between intervals 1 and 2. In contrast, the lower panel shows the strain signal from the appearance forming process increasing from $1.1 * 10^{-3}$ to $1.35 * 10^{-3}$. The strain linearity in the appearance punch head is less pronounced compared to the punching punch head, primarily due to differences in punch head shape and dimensions, as illustrated in Fig. 9. The left image in Fig. 9 shows a circular punching punch head, while the right image depicts a concave appearance punch head, highlighting the observed differences.

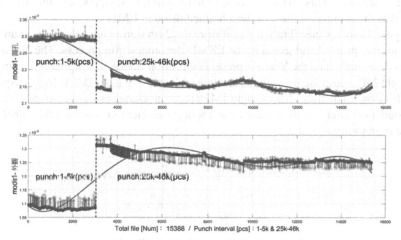

Fig. 8. Displays the strain energy charts, with the upper chart representing the values from the punching forming process, and the lower chart representing the values from the appearance forming process.

- Ensemble Empirical Mode Decomposition (EEMD): [1, 2, 3] The Hilbert-Huang Transform (HHT), proposed by Dr. Norden E. Huang and his colleagues in 1998, consists of two main steps: Empirical Mode Decomposition (EMD) and Hilbert Transform (HT). The Ensemble Empirical Mode Decomposition (EEMD) used in this study, also introduced by Dr. Norden E. Huang in 2008, aims to improve the Intrinsic Mode Functions (IMF) extracted in the EMD process.

In EMD, it is essential that both local maxima and local minima cross zero points. If an extremum does not cross a zero point, it is ignored, and the next extremum at a zero crossing is taken. This may lead to the extraction of amplitudes larger than the original signal, causing signal distortion. To prevent this distortion, EEMD adds white noise with minimal amplitude, satisfying Gaussian processes, to the time-domain signal

Fig. 9. Illustrates the schematic diagrams of the punch head dimensions, with the left diagram depicting the circular punch head for punching, and the right diagram representing the concave-shaped appearance punch head.

before processing. This creates an ensemble of multiple samples, and the true IMF is defined as the average of the samples obtained through EMD.

Figure 10 shows the vibration signal from the 24th stamping cycle in the Shunde on-site stamping process, subjected to the EEMD decomposition process. The X-axis represents data points, and the Y-axis represents vibration values. The signal is decomposed into eight IMF components, with the frequency decreasing from IMF1 (high-frequency) to IMF8 (low-frequency). These eight IMFs are considered as significant features, and after statistical analysis, they are used as input parameters to construct the punch head failure monitoring model.

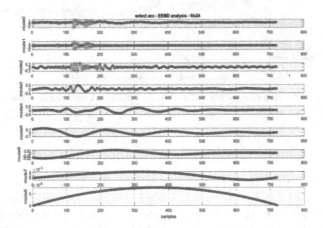

Fig. 10. EEMD Decoupling of Accelerometer Vibration Signals

Figure 11, we employ Eq. (1) to perform statistical calculations for EEMD (Ensemble Empirical Mode Decomposition) modes 1 through 8 within two distinct stamping intervals, delineated by the black dashed lines. These intervals correspond to the stamping ranges specified in Table 1, specifically, 1–5 k strokes and 25 k–46 k strokes. The X-axis in the figure represents a total of 15,410 data points of stamping records, while the Y-axis represents the vibration energy values obtained through RMS (Root Mean

Square) analysis of each stamping event. From top to bottom, the plot presents the energy values for EEMD modes 1 through 8.

Mode 1, representing the original time-domain signal, exhibits minimal differences in values between the two intervals, making it unsuitable for use as an input parameter. Modes 2 to 4, however, clearly demonstrate noticeable variations in values, rendering them highly suitable as the primary parameters for training. Modes 5 to 8 exhibit moderate differences in values and can also be employed as supplementary training data.

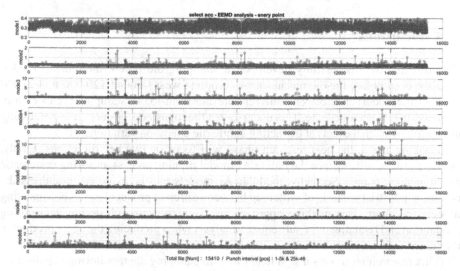

Fig. 11. Vibration Energy Representation of EEMD Mode 1 – Mode 8

- Neural Network Model (Bayesian regularization, BR): The Bayesian regularization (BR) algorithm serves as the foundation for the model used in this research, aiming to expedite the training speed of neural networks. The Bayesian regularization method is specifically designed to utilize a mean square error loss function. As mentioned in reference [7], trainbr can train neural networks as long as network weights, inputs, and transfer functions are differentiable.

Bayesian regularization minimizes the linear combination between the square error and the weights, modifying this combination to ensure the network's generalizability upon training completion, as discussed by Foresee and Hagan in reference [8]. The algorithm incorporates Bayesian regularization within the Levenberg-Marquardt optimization method. Backpropagation is employed to compute the performance gradient with respect to weights and bias variables, denoted as jX. Each variable is adjusted according to Levenberg-Marquardt as follows:

$$jj = jX * jX \, je = jX * E \, dX = -(jj + I * mu)\backslash je,$$

where E represents all error terms, I is the identity matrix, and mu is an adaptive value increased by mu_inc until the above change leads to a decrease in performance.

Subsequently, the network is updated, and mu is decreased by mu_dec. Training stops under the following conditions:

- Maximum number of training epochs is reached.
- Maximum training time is exceeded.
- Performance falls below a certain threshold.
- Performance gradient becomes smaller than min_grad.
- mu exceeds mu_max.

3 Conclusions

This research has successfully developed a stamping die failure monitoring model. Notably, even before the die reaches near-complete wear (around 120,000 to 180,000 strokes), the model can effectively differentiate data from 46,000 stamping cycles with an impressive 95% accuracy rate. This underscores the robustness of our signal processing methodology, which excels at extracting subtle die condition variations.

Looking ahead, the next research phase will focus on two key directions. Firstly, ongoing efforts will enhance the online AI model training process, ensuring systematic and dynamic updates. Secondly, modular AI models will be explored to address the common industrial scenario of switching between different product lines, where existing models fall short. This modular approach involves collecting clustering data during production and retaining it for subsequent analysis when producing the same product in the future.

This research represents a significant leap in stamping die monitoring capabilities, enabling accurate prediction of complete die lifespan, and contributing to enhanced production efficiency.

References

1. Zhidong, Z., Min, P., Yuquan, C.: Instantaneous frequency estimate for non-stationary signa. In: Fifth World Congress on Intelligent Control and Automation, vol. 4, pp. 3641–3643 (2004)
2. Ruqiang, Y., Gao, R.X.: Hilbert–Huang transform-based vibration signal analysis for machine health monitoring. IEEE Trans. Instrum. Meas. **55**, 2320–2329 (2006)
3. Yuping, Z.: Hilbert-Huang transform and marginal spectrum for detection of bearing localized defects. In: The Sixth World Congress on Intelligent Control and Automation, vol. 2, pp. 5457–5461 (2006).
4. Sari, D.Y., Wu, T.-L.: Investigation on sound signal emitted bypunching process for punch failure monitoring. In: Conference Paper Mar (2017)
5. Sari, D.Y., Wu, T.-L., Lin, B.-T.: Preliminary study for online monitoring during the punching process. Int. J. Adv. Manuf. Technol. **88**, 2275–2285 (2017)
6. Wu, T.-L., Sari, D.Y., Lin, B.-T., Chang, C.-W.: Monitoring of punch failure in micro-piercing process based on vibratory signal and logistic regression. Int. J. Adv. Manuf. Technol. **93**, 2447–2458 (2017)
7. MacKay, D.J.C.: Computation and neural systems. Neural Comput. **4**(3), 415–447 (1992)
8. Hagan F.-R.: Proceedings of the International Joint Conference on Neural Networks, June (1997)

Utilizing Skip-Gram for Restaurant Vector Creation and Its Application in the Selection of Ideal Restaurant Locations

Chih-Yung Chang[✉], Syu-Jhih Jhang, Yu-Ting Yang, Hsiang-Chuan Chang, and Yun-Jui Chang

Tamkang University, New Taipei City, Taiwan
cychang@mail.tku.edu.tw, {812410016,149190}@o365.tku.edu.tw,
142720@mail.fju.edu.tw

Abstract. Restaurant Site Selection (RSS) plays a pivotal role in the success of launching a new restaurant. The core elements of RSS encompass foot traffic and the consumption capacity potential at prospective sites. Previous studies often relied on data gleaned from social media or the Internet, utilizing statistical or machine learning methods to predict foot traffic. Nevertheless, amassing comprehensive data on foot traffic and consumption capacity proves arduous. Multiple factors, such as MRT flow, bus traffic, and business districts, contribute to foot traffic, rendering data collection complex. Similarly, quantifying consumption capacity involves variables like salary and the habits of residents and workers in the vicinity, posing data collection challenges. In contrast to prior work, this study derives proximity insights from numerous restaurant types and their locations. Employing the n-skip gram mechanism from natural language processing, restaurant vectors are generated for each restaurant type. These vectors subtly encapsulate information about foot traffic and consumption capacity. Subsequently, the algorithm utilizes these Restaurant Vectors to recommend optimal restaurant locations. Performance assessments confirm that the generated Restaurant Vectors effectively encompass features related to foot traffic and consumption capacity.

Keywords: n-skip gram · neural network · restaurant vector · people flow · consumption capacity · restaurant site selection

1 Introduction

The modern job market is witnessing a shift, with more individuals opting for entrepreneurship, particularly in the restaurant industry. This trend underscores the importance of meticulous planning and evaluation, with the choice of restaurant location taking center stage as a critical initial step.

Technology has revolutionized this process. In the past, information was gleaned from traditional media sources, with limited interaction between consumers and businesses. However, the advent of the internet, coupled with 5G location-aware services,

© ICST Institute for Computer Sciences, Social Informatics and Telecommunications Engineering 2024
Published by Springer Nature Switzerland AG 2024. All Rights Reserved
D.-J. Deng and J.-C. Chen (Eds.): SGIoT 2023, LNICST 557, pp. 141–147, 2024.
https://doi.org/10.1007/978-3-031-55976-1_14

has transformed the landscape. People now access the internet effortlessly through various devices, leaving digital footprints that generate a wealth of data. This social data offers invaluable insights for restaurant owners, aiding in site selection and enhancing operational efficiency.

Traditionally, site selection relied on manual data collection and statistical methods. However, artificial intelligence (AI) has emerged as a powerful tool for collecting and analyzing vast online data. Researchers have begun harnessing AI techniques, including machine and deep learning, to predict optimal restaurant locations with greater accuracy.

This paper builds upon previous AI methods, aiming to address existing challenges. It recognizes that restaurants on the same street share similar features, such as foot traffic and consumption capacity. Leveraging neighbor relations, restaurant vectors are constructed and used to identify the best street for a new restaurant. This innovative approach enhances the accuracy of site selection, offering valuable contributions through the algorithm.

1. **Restaurant Vector Construction:** This paper creates restaurant vectors to capture semantic neighboring relations between restaurants, encompassing foot traffic and consumption capacity.
2. **Data Collection Challenges Overcome:** The study sidesteps data collection difficulties regarding foot traffic and consumption capacity by relying on restaurant relationships instead.
3. **Restaurant Vector Validation:** The study validates restaurant vectors by confirming alignment with the average-person concept regarding restaurant location.

2   Related Work

Numerous studies have aimed to identify ideal business locations, utilizing various data sources including geography, movement, social data, and online government records. Some explored common factors affecting business success [2], while others incorporated machine learning techniques with carefully chosen features or advanced deep learning methods.

Researchers have expanded their focus beyond economic factors, realizing they are not the sole determinants of sound business location decisions. While early studies emphasized cost minimization and profit maximization, globalization and regulatory changes have highlighted the importance of noneconomic factors such as place image, brand, visual appeal, reputation, sense of place, and identity in decision-making. These factors, along with economic data, have become valuable inputs for recent advances in machine learning and deep learning [3].

While machine learning has its merits, it sometimes requires expert knowledge of predetermined features [7, 8, 10–12]. Consequently, some researchers turn to deep learning, which excels with abundant input data. Data sources like user-generated reviews from platforms like Yelp [1], movement data, and geographic features offer rich data for deep learning models. These approaches often outperform traditional proximity-based methods and contribute to practical tools for selecting optimal locations, as demonstrated in this paper.

3   The Proposed Model

To address previous technological limitations, this study introduces a shop location selection system consisting of a store word vector model, a street database, and a processor. The street database contains various street data, each with multiple store data entries, each specifying a store category. The store word vector model associates a word vector with each store category. The processor functions to evaluate recommendation scores for each street data based on the store categories in the street database and a target category. Subsequently, it provides location recommendations based on these scores.

The study also presents a store word vector model training method, involving the processor categorizing store data in multiple street data entries to derive various store categories. Then, the processor trains word vectors for each street data entry based on the store categories within it, establishing the store word vector model. This approach leverages the concept of word vectors, where the similarity between store categories implies a higher likelihood of co-location in the same street. Thus, users, when seeking a location for opening a shop, can set a target category. The shop location selection system utilizes the target category, the store word vector model, and the street database to suggest suitable streets for the target category, offering users valuable guidance for their shop location decisions.

To address this, our research presents a location selection system comprising a Store Word Vector Model, a Street Database, and a Processor. The Street Database holds data from various streets, with each street containing store data categorized by store type. The Store Word Vector Model generates word vectors based on store categories. The Processor utilizes this data to determine recommendation scores for each street based on the store categories in the Street Database and a target category. It then offers location suggestions. Our approach starts by collecting store data from multiple streets, obtained from sources like government records, public data, and Google Maps. This data serves as a reference for store categories, encompassing store names, product information, and services offered. The Processor classifies store data within street entries to derive diverse store categories. Semantic analysis tools, such as Natural Language Processing (NLP), may assist in understanding products or services based on store names. Classification can also consider factors like product types or service categories. In cases where store names are ambiguous, predefined data or manual classification can be applied. In some scenarios, the analysis focuses solely on stores within the same industry, such as food services or clothing. For instance, when used for restaurant site selection, only food-related businesses within street data are categorized based on their product types.

Furthermore, store classification may extend to multiple industries within the same street data. This approach enables word vector analysis across different categories. Additionally, stores can be categorized by price variations for the same products or services. For example, high-end and budget-friendly versions of the same store category can be differentiated, offering granularity in categorization. After classification, each store category is encoded numerically for subsequent processing, making use of methods like one-hot encoding. This approach streamlines location selection by leveraging word vectors to assess the suitability of streets for a target category, enhancing the decision-making process.

The processor trains restaurant word vectors based on restaurant categories within the same street data. Word vectors represent word relationships in a vector space, where closer vectors indicate frequent co-occurrence. Similarly, when restaurant categories often coexist on a street, their word vectors become close.

Various methods like BERT, GPT, ELMO, or word2vec are used to train these vectors. In some cases, the processor selects one category from the same street and another from the opposite side for training. For instance, if there are three adjacent categories like tea shops, bento shops, and dessert shops, training can involve bento shops with tea shops and dessert shops.

The processor calculates the similarity between the target category and restaurant categories. The results are summed for each street, producing recommendation scores. These scores rank streets for potential restaurant locations, helping users make site selection decisions.

The following formula (1) is used to calculate the association between the target category and the restaurant category, where π_i represents the vector of the target category, and π_j represents the vector of the restaurant category. The result of this formula falls between −1 and 1. A value of 1 indicates a high association between the target category and the restaurant category when the two vectors have the same direction. Conversely, a value of −1 suggests a very low association when the vectors point in opposite directions.

$$\text{Sim}(\pi_i, \pi_j) = \frac{\pi_i . \pi_j}{\|\pi_i\|\|\pi_j\|} \tag{1}$$

In Fig. 1, let's delve into our proposed _Restaurant Vector Creation_ (RVC) algorithm, guided by the aforementioned design principles. Initially, s_i represents a certain street. Each street $s_i = \{a_{i,1}, a_{i,2} \ldots, a_{i,|s_i|}\}$ is composed of several existing restaurants $a_{i,j}$. Each s_i is evaluated to calculate its $score_i$, signifying its suitability as the target location. In step 1, each street s_i in the set S undergoes steps 2 to 12. In step 2, each street s_i has initial value $score_i = 0$.

Given a restaurant a_{target}, step 3 aims to develop a location selection mechanism, which determines the location of the restaurant a_{target} to open a shop. Consider each restaurant $a_{i,j} \in S$ and execute the operations outlined in steps 5 to 12. In steps 5 to 7, street s_i earns points if A_k is not equal to A_{target}, indicating that $a_{i,j}$ and a_{target} belong to different restaurant categories. The points awarded are determined by the similarity of the restaurant vectors between $a_{i,j}$ and a_{target}, denoted as $\text{Sim}(\pi_{target}, \pi_k)$. Conversely, if A_k equals A_{target} ($A_k = A_{target}$), street s_i loses points due to the competition between similar restaurants within the same street.

Steps 8 to 12 correspond to the above-mentioned operations. To ensure fairness given varying numbers of restaurants on different streets, step 10 normalizes the $score_i$ by the number of restaurants on the street s_i. Ultimately, the street with the highest score is recommended as the optimal location for the restaurant a_{target}.

Algorithm: *Restaurant-Vector Creation(RVC)*	
Input: The target street a_{target}	
Output: The best location s_{best} in region R.	
1.	for each s_i in S:
2.	$\{$ $score_i = 0$;
3.	$n_i = 0$;
4.	for each $a_{i,j}$ in s_i:
5.	$\{$let $A_k = g(a_{i,j})$;
6.	if $A_k \neq A_{target}$:
7.	$temp = Sim(\pi_{target}, \pi_k)$
8.	if $temp \geq \lambda$:
9.	$score_i = score_i + temp$
10.	$n_i + +$;
11.	$\}$
12.	$score_i = (score_i / n_i)$ $\}$
13.	$s_{best} = arg \max_{s_i \in S} score_i$
14.	

Fig. 1. The *RVC* Street Recommend Algorithm.

4 Performance Evaluation

This section evaluates the performance of the *RVC*(Restaurant Vector Creation) algorithm in comparison to the People Flow algorithm for restaurant site selection. The People Flow algorithm relies on data like MRT stations, bus stops, business districts, schools, office buildings, and parks to identify suitable restaurant locations. In contrast, RVC uses an RCNN network to assign each restaurant category a vector, trained based on the relations between neighboring restaurants on the same street. The similarity between these vectors determines the frequency of neighboring restaurants.

Figure 2 primarily compares the performance of the proposed RCNN with the existing People Flow Algorithm, focusing on accuracy, prediction, and recall metrics. RCNN(λ) denotes the RCNN performance achieved by setting a threshold value λ, with RCNN(0.8), RCNN(0.6), and RCNN(0.4) representing performances using λ values of 0.8, 0.6, and 0.4, respectively. The People Flow Algorithm recommends streets based on collected information related to People Flow, such as the count of individuals entering/exiting MRT and bus stations, and the number of convenience stores, among other factors.

The experiments vary the number of neurons from 1 to 4 and the number of streets from 100 to 800. Results consistently show that the performance of the three RCNN mechanisms improves with the increasing number of streets in terms of accuracy, precision, and recall. This improvement is attributed to the larger dataset, allowing the RCNN network to extract better relations from neighboring restaurants, resulting in enhanced accuracy, precision, and recall. Conversely, the accuracy, precision, and recall of the existing People Flow algorithm remain constant and are lower than those of the proposed *RVC*(*Restaurant Vector Creation*) algorithm.

Furthermore, the three RCNN mechanisms achieve the highest accuracy, prediction, and recall when the number of neurons is set to two. This is because increasing the number

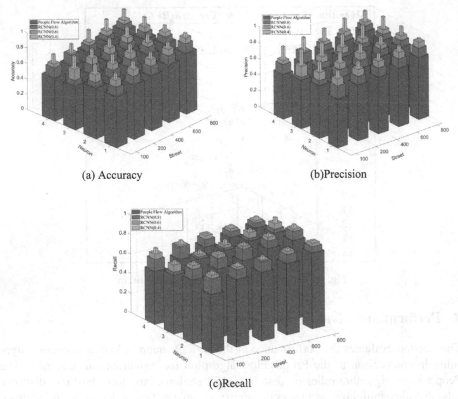

(a) Accuracy   (b)Precision

(c)Recall

Fig. 2. Performance of two compared algorithms and three weights of *RVC* in terms of accuracy, precision and recall.

of neurons spreads the values of the restaurant vectors across more dimensions, reducing cosine similarity comparisons and, consequently, accuracy, precision, and recall.

In contrast, the proposed *RVC* algorithm outperforms the traditional People Flow algorithm in all scenarios. This superiority stems from the People Flow algorithm's inability to collect complete information affecting accuracy, precision, and recall, particularly regarding consumption-related factors like housing prices and people's salaries. In contrast, RVC leverages relations within neighboring restaurant information and represents them using restaurant vectors. These vectors encompass all features impacting restaurant openings, resulting in the superior performance of *RVC* over the People Flow Algorithm.

5   Conclusions

This paper delves into the relationships between neighboring restaurants to create restaurant vectors, which carry the semantic meaning that closer vectors of two restaurant categories suggest they are frequently found on the same street. Restaurants located on the same street often share common characteristics, including foot traffic and consumption capacity. Utilizing restaurant vectors to identify the best-suited street, with features similar to the target restaurant, can encompass all the implicit attributes that influence the restaurant business. Instead of the arduous task of collecting comprehensive data on foot traffic and consumption capacity, the restaurant vector offers a solution.

To our knowledge, the concept of a restaurant vector signifies the similarity of the target restaurant. The novel aspect of our proposed *RVC(Restaurant Vector Creation)* algorithm lies in its ability to generate restaurant vectors for each restaurant category and employ them to recommend suitable locations for opening new restaurants. We believe that restaurant vectors hold the potential for broader applications in the restaurant industry. Experimental results affirm that *RVC* surpasses traditional algorithms that rely on data collected from social media or the internet and predict foot traffic using statistical or machine learning methods.

References

1. Tayeen, A.S., Mtibaa, A., Misra, S.: Location, location, location! In: IEEE/ACM International Conference on Advances in Social Networks Analysis and Mining (2019)
2. Dixit, A., Clouse, C., Turken, N.: Strategic business location decisions: importance of economic factors and place image. Rutgers Bus. Rev. **4** (2019)
3. Bilen, T., .Erel-Ozcevik, M., Yaslan, Y., Oktug, S.F.: A smart city application: business location estimator using machine learning techniques. In: IEEE International Conference on High-Performance Computing and Communications (2018)
4. Bhole, J., Nandiyawar, S., Pawar, S., Vora, P.: Smart site selection using machine learning. Int. Res. J. Eng. Technol. **7**(5), 3012–3015 (2020)
5. .Mazhi, K.Z., Suryana, L.E., Davi, A., Dewi, W.R.: Site selection of retail shop based on spatial analysis and machine learning. In: International Conference on Advanced Computer Science and Information Systems (ICACSIS) (2020)
6. Han, S., Jia, X., Chen, X., Gupta, S., Kumar, A., Lin, Z.: Search well and be wise: a machine learning approach to search for a profitable location. J. Bus. Res. **144**, 416–427 (2022)
7. Eravci, W.R., Bulut, N., Etemoglu, C., Ferhatosmanoglu, H.: Location recommendations for new businesses using check-in data. In: IEEE 16th International Conference on Data Mining Workshops (ICDMW), pp. 1110–1117 (2016)
8. Chang, T.-H.: Restaurant location selection by utilizing the fuzzy preference relations. In: IEEE International Conference on Industrial Engineering and Engineering Management (2010)
9. Wang, Y., Li, S., Zhang, X., Jiang, D., Hao, M., Zhou, R.: Site selection of digital signage in Beijing: a combination of machine learning and an empirical approach. Int. J. Geo-Inf. **9**(4), 3012–3015 (2020)
10. Furtado, A.S., Fileto, R., Renso, C.: Assessing the attractiveness of places with movement data. J. Inf. Data Manag. **4**, 124–133 (2013)
11. Quan, X., Wenyin, L., Dou, W., Xiong, H., Ge, Y.: Link graph analysis for business site selection. Computer **45**(3), 64–69 (2012)
12. Wang, F., Chen, L., Pan, W.: Where to place your next restaurant? Optimal restaurant placement via leveraging user-generated reviews. In: The 25th ACM International on Conference on Information and Knowledge Management (2016)

Load Balancing Algorithm
in a Software-Defined Network
Environment with Round Robin
and Least Connections

Chandra Wijaya[1,2], Rita Wiryasaputra[1,3], Chin-Yin Huang[1],
Jodi Tanato[2], and Chao-Tung Yang[4,5]($\boxtimes$)

[1] Department of Industrial Engineering and Enterprise Information,
Tunghai University, Taichung 407224, Taiwan
huangcy@go.thu.edu.tw
[2] Department of Informatics, Parahyangan Catholic University,
Bandung 40141, Indonesia
chandraw@unpar.ac.id
[3] Department of Informatics, Krida Wacana Christian University,
Jakarta 11470, Indonesia
rita.wiryasaputra@ukrida.ac.id
[4] Department of Computer Science, Tunghai University, Taichung 407224, Taiwan
ctyang@thu.edu.tw
[5] Research Center for Smart Sustainable Circular Economy, Tunghai University,
Taichung 407224, Taiwan

Abstract. In a traditional computer network, each device has its configuration. The Software Defined Network (SDN) architecture ensures that
every device in the network will become a dummy device, which must
connect to a controller before action can be taken on every packet that
the device receives. Each device does not require manual configuration
with the centralized configuration. The huge growth of internet traffic can
affect the server's performance when handling requests of many clients.
The algorithms, such as Round Robin and Least Connection, influence
the load-balancing technology to divide the request to some servers. The
server's performance increases after implementing load balancing with
the algorithm in testing. The comparative result of the Round Robin
and Least Connection algorithms shows that the Least Connection performs better than the Round Robin algorithm. By using load balancing
in the SDN architecture, the increasing of the request capacity can be
handled by the server.

Keywords: SDN · load balancing · least connection · round robin ·
Openflow

1 Introduction

The functionality of traditional intermediary network devices is the control and
data planes. The control plane is an entity that controls network packets from

© ICST Institute for Computer Sciences, Social Informatics and Telecommunications Engineering 2024
Published by Springer Nature Switzerland AG 2024. All Rights Reserved
D.-J. Deng and J.-C. Chen (Eds.): SGIoT 2023, LNICST 557, pp. 148–157, 2024.
https://doi.org/10.1007/978-3-031-55976-1_15

a source device until it reaches the destination device. The data plane sends the packets using the path determined by the control plane. In a traditional network, each intermediary device controls its control and data planes. In a Software Defined Network (SDN), the control functions are located on a centralized controller. SDN refers to designing and managing network packets in which each device's control plane and data plane are separated [11]. The control plane will be handled by one or more controller(s). The intermediary devices will handle the data plane function that moves a packet from the inbound port to the outbound port, according to the rules given by the controller. Rapid technological developments support sustainable development goals. The Internet of Things (IoT) is a technology that is commonly used to capture data from sensors, store it and then analyze the data for specific needs. The IOT has numerous applications such as in agriculture and aquaculture management, air quality monitoring, water resources monitoring [7]. As more and more sensors are being used, bigger data is generated by the sensors hence requiring increasingly large storage resources over time. Big data is a technology for storing large amounts of data, up to the terabyte scale. Several important aspects of big data technology include scalability, reliability, and efficiency to support large amounts of data [1,9,10]. The growth of internet users forces the server to process client requests rapidly without dropping the requests, even if it is in large quantities. A technique to increase the capacity of the server is load balancing which works by dividing client requests and forwarding it into a group of the same functionality servers. After being processed by the server, the reply is sent back to the clients without the clients knowing which server is responding to their requests. Some algorithms for load balancing techniques include Round Robin, Weighted Round Robin, Least Connection, and Resource Based. Some examples of load balancing technology are Hadoop and Ceph which are distributed storage systems that provide scalable, reliable, and fault-tolerant data storage that supports high-performance data transactions [8]. This research compares the Round Robin and Least Connection algorithms regarding the load balancing implementation in the SDN Controller environment. The paper is structured as follows: the first section reviews the research background, Sect. 2 describes the previous research relevant to this research, Sect. 3 presents the research methodology, and the experiment and conclusions are outlined in Sects. 4 and Sect. 5, respectively.

2   Related Works

Nugroho [2] conducted the performance test on both traditional network infrastructure and a network with SDN infrastructure. Two scenarios were used for the test: the network with and without any generated traffic that loads from 20 Mbps to 100 Mbps. Using Wireshark as a packet capture application and analyzer, the researchers concluded that a network utilizing Software-Defined Networking (SDN) exhibits significantly improved performance compared to a traditional network in terms of reduced latency, decreased delay, increased throughput, and lower packet loss. Pramono [3] implemented HAProxy and Nginx for load balancing servers using the Least Connection approach. Each server's load balancing will be tested with the same parameter values. Using the Apache JMeter and Apache Benchmark as stress test tools, the test shows a significant difference in throughput (requests/minute) when the leastconn algorithm is used instead of the Round Robin algorithm. Saumendu [5] explained that load balancing allocates the workloads evenly to all the nodes with the purpose of improving the entire system's performance. Tasks come from various clients and are received and distributed along the servers. Different load balancing algorithms measure various testing metric parameters such as response time, throughput, optimizing resource utilization, ability to handle faulty conditions, migration time, and scalability. Rana [4] discussed the challenges of SDN, namely reliability, scalability, low-level interface, performance, and security. Reliability is essential for SDN to validate network management and handle any system failures as it must perform automatic fault detection and then, reroute the traffic to achieve reliability. A feature of SDN is scalability which is the ability to handle the growth of a system, network, or process during daily events. A low-level interface means that the SDN translates a policy into a low-level configuration for the network switches. The SDN framework must be able to translate and coordinate the multiple asynchronous events at the switch. The performance and security of SDN networks may be compromised due to the open interface which can introduce new types of network attacks and degrade the overall performance of the SDN. POX is a Python-based open-source SDN controller used to increase the development and prototyping of network applications; a POX controller comes with mininet. It has several scripts that can be developed further such as DHCP service, layer2 and layer3 forwarding service, network discovery, and many more [6].

3   Methodology

Figure 1 illustrates the overall research stages. To create the network simulation, the infrastructure virtualization employed a Linux machine. Based on the framework, the mininet and the SDN controller were used in the framework. The next stage was the network topology where some nodes played roles as clients and others as servers. The controller and the switches interconnecting the nodes were created to manage all traffic in the network. After the configuration, the Round Robin algorithm and the Least Connection were evaluated with the httperf software that can measure the total requests handled (connection rate/second) and total packet loss of each algorithm. The packet loss and throughput parameters were used as the benchmark to determine the best approach.

4   Experiment

This section explains the implementation of the proposed model. The Hypervisor Oracle Virtual Box was used to create the virtual machine. The operating system was a precompiled Ubuntu Linux, including the SDN Controller and all the required software. The research topology employed the load balancing of

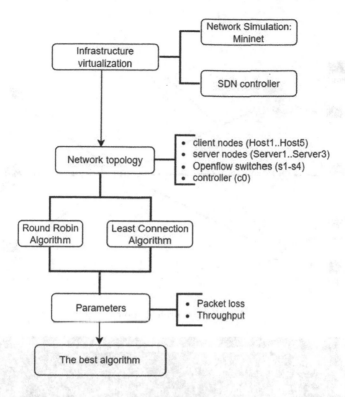

Fig. 1. Research Methodology

client requests to multiple servers, shown in Fig. 2. There were 5 nodes as the clients with the name Host1 until Host5, and 3 servers, namely: server1, server2, and server3, which handled the client requests. A set of switches (s1-s4) also established interconnections among these nodes. The node c0 was designated as the controller responsible for managing all network traffic. In SDN, the switch must support the Openflow protocol which is the protocol used to communicate between the switch and the controller. As such, the network management can be centralized in one controller. In this research, Openvswitch, an Openflow-enabled virtual switch, was used. A virtual switch refers to the capability of forwarding data packets between virtual machines. A virtual switch can forward data packets from a virtual machine to the physical network. Openvswitch can be programmed and controlled by Openflow and OpenvSwitch Database (OVSDB). The SDN Controller utilized in this study is POX, an open-source and openflow-based controller. POX runs in Command Line Interface (CLI), thus lacking any graphical interface. Figure 3 shows the directory structure of the POX SDN Controller. The directory comprises numerous Python scripts. Users might modify or add controller features by modifying or adding the scripts in this directory. These modified or added scripts can then be called when the user runs the POX Controller. In this study, there are two algorithms implemented, specifi-

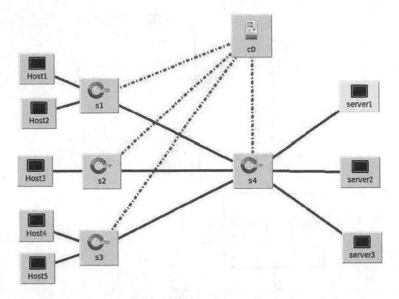

Fig. 2. Research Topology

```
joditanato@joditanato-VirtualBox: ~/pox/pox/misc

joditanato@joditanato-VirtualBox:-$ cd pox
joditanato@joditanato-VirtualBox:-/pox$ ls
debug-pox.py   ext   LICENSE   NOTICE   pox   pox.py   README.md   setup.cfg   tests   tools
joditanato@joditanato-VirtualBox:-/pox$ cd pox/forwarding/
joditanato@joditanato-VirtualBox:-/pox/pox/forwarding$ ls
hub.py          l2_flowvisor.py  l2_multi.py  l2_nx_self_learning.py  l3_learning.py
__init__.py     l2_learning.py   l2_nx.py     l2_pairs.py             topo_proactive.py
joditanato@joditanato-VirtualBox:-/pox/pox/forwarding$ cd ..
joditanato@joditanato-VirtualBox:-/pox/pox$ cd misc/
joditanato@joditanato-VirtualBox:-/pox/pox/misc$ ls
cbench.py       __init__.py       nat.py          poxpdb.py
full_payload.py ip_loadbalancer.py of_tutorial.py  telnetd
gephi_topo.py   mac_blocker.py    pidfile.py      tweak.py
joditanato@joditanato-VirtualBox:-/pox/pox/misc$
```

Fig. 3. POX Directory Structure

cally Round Robin and Least Connection. The flowchart for each algorithm is shown in Fig. 4a, and Fig. 4b. To test the implementation of the load balancing algorithm, the virtual server is added to serve the client requests. When the controller receives the data packet, it will forward the packet to several servers with different IP addresses. The server which responds to the request is automatically chosen by the controller using the load balancing algorithm. Figure 5 depicts the ip of the virtual servers available and which server would respond to the data packet forwarded by the controller. Each server will respond to each one of the data packets sent to them. After testing the connectivity with the virtual server is succeeded, mininet can also emulate the webserver so the load balanc-

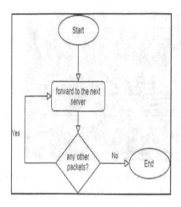
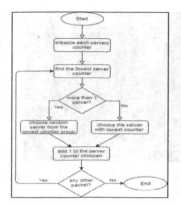

(a) Round Robin Algorithm   (b) Least Connection Algorithm

Fig. 4. The Flowchart

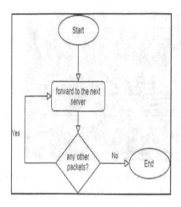

Fig. 5. Testing the Load Balancing Algorithm using Virtual Server

ing algorithm can be conducted. The command "python -m SimpleHTTPServer 80" emulates those webservers. The command instructs the host to run Python script, which runs simple webserver and bind the service to port 80 (http). In the Fig. 6a, shown the node server1, which represents webserver listened on port 80. Figure 6b shows Host1 trying to access the webserver from the Host1 interface by using CURL command. To benchmark the algorithm and the SDN controller, the httperf software was used to simulate an HTTP request and record the total requests, total responses, total errors, the total time needed to test the average/minimum/maximum time needed for the total request, requests sent per second, and replies sent per second. The httperf showed the total requests handled (connection rate/second) and total packet loss of each algorithm. As shown in Fig. 2, there are three servers assigned to handle the requests from the clients.

(a) Mininet host running simple webserver   (b) Host1 try to access the web server using CURL

Fig. 6. Simple Webserver Implementation and Testing

Using the httperf, the experiment sent 100 requests, 200 requests, 300 requests, 400 requests, and 500 requests from clients node Host1, Host2, Host3, Host4, Host5. All requests addressed to the main server will be distributed to the backline servers, according to the algorithm used by the controller. Figure 7 shows the experiment of sending 100 requests from Host1 clients resulting in a connection rate of 44.6 connection/s and the clients received 78 replies, thus, the packet loss rate is 22%. Figure 8 features the experiment of sending 500 requests from the Host5 client to the main server in which the connection rate decreased to only 29.1 connection/s and the client received 471 packets replied hence the packet loss rate is 5,8%. The testing results for the Round Robin Algorithm and the Least Connection algorithm are shown in Table 1. Figure 9 shows the comparison of throughput (in conn/s) between the Round Robin algorithm and the Least Connection algorithm. The performance of the Round Robin algorithm decreases in line with the increase in the requests. However, in the Least Connection algorithm, the performance is stable with a range of 32.52 and 34.00 although the requests are increasing. This means the Least Connection algorithm is better in terms of throughput. Based on the parameter packet loss in the Round Robin algorithm, its packet loss increases in line with the increase of the requests. Even though the Least Connection algorithm experienced a packet loss increase like the Round Robin algorithm, its packet loss has a lower percentage compared to the Round Robin algorithm. The comparison of packet loss from both algorithms is shown in Fig. 10. The algorithm's ideal performance is the algorithm with the lower percentage of packet loss.

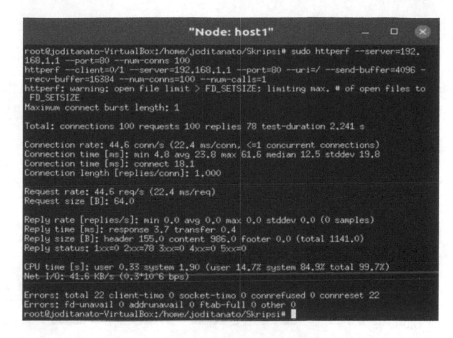

Fig. 7. Sending 100 requests from node Host1

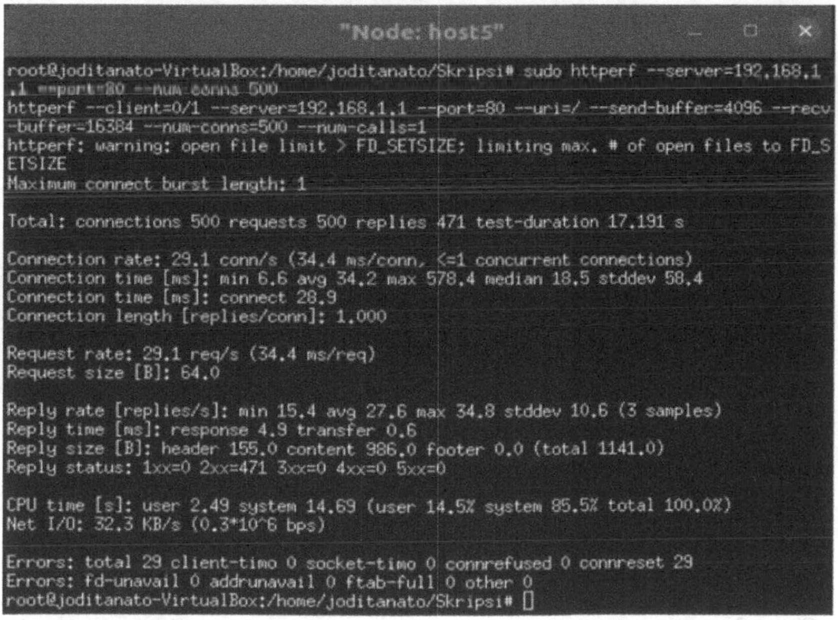

Fig. 8. Sending 100 requests from node Host5

Table 1. Test Result

Request	Round Robin		Least Connection	
	Avg. Conn/s	Avg. Packet Loss (%)	Avg. Conn/s	Avg. Packet Loss (%)
100	40.96	15.20	32.70	10.60
200	34.90	17.20	33.44	11.10
300	33.94	20.67	32.62	12.27
400	32.06	23.30	34.00	15.25
500	29.66	29.40	32.52	17.64

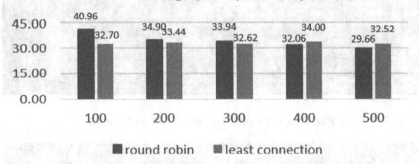

Fig. 9. Throughput Comparison

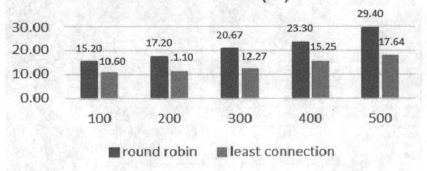

Fig. 10. Packet Loss Comparison

5   Conclusion

The implementation of SDN offers several advantages to processing network packets. Tracking each packet and which route is chosen to forward the packet is possible. The benefits of using an SDN controller are that network management can be centralized compared to traditional network management. In terms of increasing network server performance, the load balancing algorithm can be used to improve the network performance, which forwards the requests coming to the server pool. Load balancing distributes the load into several servers, thus, improving the service's reliability since the average throughput can be higher, and the packet loss can be minimized. With the implementation of a load balancing algorithm in the SDN controller, the comparison shows that the least connection algorithm is better than the Round Robin algorithm in terms of throughput (conn/s) and average packet loss.

Acknowledgement. This research was supported in part by the National Science and Technology Council (NSTC), Taiwan R.O.C. grants numbers 112-2622-E-029-003,112-2621-M-029-004, and 110-2221-E-029-020-MY3.

References

1. Chang, C.-H., Jiang, F.-C., Yang, C.-T., Chou, S.-C.: On construction of a big data warehouse accessing platform for campus power usages. J. Parallel Distrib. Comput. **133**, 40–50 (2019)
2. Nugroho, H., Irfan, M., Faruq, A.: Software defined networks: a comparative study and quality of services evaluation. Sci. J. Inform. **6**(2), 181–192 (2019)
3. Pramono, L., Cokro, R., Waskito, Y.: Round-robin algorithm in HAProxy and Nginx load balancing performance evaluation: a review, pp. 367–372 (2018)
4. Rana, D.S., Dhondiyal, S.A., Chamoli, S.K.: Software defined networking (SDN) challenges, issues and solution. Int. J. Comput. Sci. Eng. **7**(1), 884–889 (2019)
5. Roy, S., Hossain, D.M.A., Sen, S.K., Hossain, N., Al Asif, M.R.: Measuring the performance on load balancing algorithms. Global J. Comput. Sci. Technol. **19**, 41–49 (2019)
6. Tok, M.S., Demirci, M.: Security analysis of SDN controller-based DHCP services and attack mitigation with DHCPguard. Comput. Secur. **109**, 102394 (2021)
7. Wiryasaputra, R., Huang, C.Y., Kristiani, E., Liu, P.Y., Yeh, T.K., Yang, C.T.: Review of an intelligent indoor environment monitoring and management system for covid-19 risk mitigation. Front. Public Health **10**, 1022055 (2023)
8. Yang, C.-T., Chen, C.-J., Tsan, Y.-T., Liu, P.-Y., Chan, Y.-W., Chan, W.-C.: An implementation of real-time air quality and influenza-like illness data storage and processing platform. Comput. Hum. Behav. **100**, 266–274 (2019)
9. Yang, C.-T., Chen, H.-W., Chang, E.-J., Kristiani, E., Nguyen, K.L.P., Chang, J.-S.: Current advances and future challenges of AIoT applications in particulate matters (PM) monitoring and control. J. Hazard. Mater. **419**, 126442 (2021)
10. Yang, C.-T., Chen, S.-T., Den, W., Wang, Y.-T., Kristiani, E.: Implementation of an intelligent indoor environmental monitoring and management system in cloud. Futur. Gener. Comput. Syst. **96**, 731–749 (2019)
11. Yang, C.-T., Chen, S.-T., Liu, J.-C., Yang, Y.-Y., Mitra, K., Ranjan, R.: Implementation of a real-time network traffic monitoring service with network functions virtualization. Futur. Gener. Comput. Syst. **93**, 687–701 (2019)

Author Index

© ICST Institute for Computer Sciences, Social Informatics and Telecommunications Engineering 2024
Published by Springer Nature Switzerland AG 2024. All Rights Reserved
D.-J. Deng and J.-C. Chen (Eds.): SGIoT 2023, LNICST 557, p. 159, 2024.
https://doi.org/10.1007/978-3-031-55976-1

Printed in the United States
by Baker & Taylor Publisher Services